UP-COUNTRY SWAHILI
EXERCISES

FOR THE SOLDIER, SETTLER, MINER,
MERCHANT, AND THEIR WIVES

AND FOR ALL WHO DEAL WITH UP-COUNTRY NATIVES
WITHOUT INTERPRETERS

BY

F. H. LE BRETON

British Library Cataloguing-in-Publication Data
A catalogue record for this book is available from
the British Library

PREFACE

At the end of the first World War the Author decided to retire from the army and to become a Soldier Settler in Kenya.

He was informed that the best book from which to learn Swahili was " Bishop Steere's Swahili Exercises ". He accordingly bought a copy and went through it very thoroughly, learning every vocabulary, sixteen words at a time, and writing out every exercise more than once.

During the voyage to Mombasa, on S.S. "Carisbrook Castle, " he shared a table with some Kenya Officials who gave him an oral examination on his Swahili.

He passed with flying colours, but he was amazed when the Chief Examiner said, " Yes, you know it very well, but of course you won't be able to use that sort of Swahili on your farm! "

" What do you mean ? " asked the Author.

" Oh! " replied the Examiner, " that is all Coastal Swahili, they don't understand all that complicated grammar up-country!"

The Author was flabbergasted. " Well, . . .! . . .!! " he cried, " what the . . . . . . have I been wasting all my time for in learning a sort of Swahili that is not generally understood on a farm! Why on earth doesn't someone write a book of the type of Swahili that they will understand ? "

The Chief Examiner shrugged his shoulders. " Nobody ever has," he said, " and I don't suppose anybody ever will."

The Author waited for fifteen years for someone else to write a book on the sort of Swahili that all normal Europeans and Natives talk, except at the Coast, but as no one did—he had to do it himself.

Here it is.

A

INTRODUCTION

Correct Swahili is a very complicated language native to Zanzibar and the coastal belt of East Africa.

To the ordinary up-country native, Swahili is a foreign language, of which he possesses only a very limited knowledge.

This book aims at teaching, in a simple way, just that degree of Swahili that is understood and talked by the average intelligent up-country native.

All previous Swahili books have dealt with correct coastal Swahili, but the average up-country native definitely does not understand the intricacies of correct Swahili, neither does any settler, miner, business man, or wife ever attempt to speak it to him, and the official deals with him largely through interpreters into his own dialect.

In any case of doubt as to what degree of correctness to employ, I have inclined towards the more correct forms, and I have indicated in " italics " the correct form of speech in those cases in which the usual form is different.

In up-country Swahili many English words are used. For the sake of uniformity I have spelt these as a native would spell them, in conformance with the few very simple rules of pronunciation.

The number of English words in use is on the increase, and if a student is short of a word he should try the English. It may be understood !

Conversely, if he is confronted with an unknown Swahili word that is not to be found in any vocabulary, he should consider whether it may not be a distorted form of some English word.

Common forms of distortion are indicated on Page 46.

Up-country Swahili no doubt varies slightly in different parts of East Africa, and each district may use a few words taken from the language of the local tribe. These have been excluded, as they are not universal.

The extent of the vocabulary of an up-country native is very limited, so English sentences for translation must be simplified to conform.

Solutions of the exercises will be found at the end of the book.

There are a few cases in which the Solutions show slight variations from the forms given in the text, in these cases either form may be used.

While the Swahili Vocabulary, Pages 56—73, contains, in about 1,500 words, all that are considered necessary for a full knowledge of Up-Country Swahili, yet these can be translated into probably four or five times as many English words. How many words are there in an English Dictionary ? Many, many thousands! It is therefore impossible in a book of this size to include in the English-Swahili Vocabulary, Pages 74—86, all the words that the new-comer may think of translating into Swahili; for that purpose I would recommend Madan's English-Swahili Dictionary, though many words therein would not be understood by the Up-Country Native.

In the above-mentioned Swahili Vocabulary some five hundred of the commonest Swahili words have been marked with an asterisk, and I would advise a beginner to read these through four or five times, and pick out the words that he wishes to learn first, for daily use, before he can plod through the exercises, which is, of course, the best way whereby to learn the language.

F. H. Le B.

ENDEBESS,
    JUNE, 1955

CONTENTS.

UP-COUNTRY SWAHILI.

PRONUNCIATION.

In Swahili the vowels are pronounced as in Italian and the consonants as in English.[1]

To get the correct vowel sounds drop the " H " in the following English words.

A as the vowel sound of Ha ! or as in Hard
E ,, ,, ,, ,, ,, Hay
I ,, ,, ,, ,, ,, He
O ,, ,, ,, ,, ,, Hoe[2]
U ,, ,, ,, ,, ,, Who

The accent is always on the one-from-last vowel.[3]

Read the following sentences according to the above rules, if they are used correctly the result will give you English sentences.

Thiz tu kaz a veri chip. Hu me yu bi pliz ? Hau nais yu a luking tudei, so brait, so ge. Thi stej koch kem kwait sun. Sneks a had tu si. Thi pul sims dip. Pita gev mi mai ti tu let. E snowi de meks mi kold, e stov tu hit thi rum wud bi gud.

---

[1] " CH " and " TH " are used as in English. " G " is always hard. " C," " Q " and " X " having no individual sounds of their own are not used, except " C " in " Ch."

[2] " O " has rather more the sound of " Aw " as in " Law " than has the ordinary English " O."

[3] Sometimes an extra vowel has to be added in order to keep this rule inviolate, e.g., Kioo=looking-glass. The second " O " is hardly heard, but its presence moves the accent on to the " O " instead of allowing it to fall on the " I " as it would have to do if written with only one " O."

Learn the following :—

Jambo	..	How d'you do !	Bwana	..	Sir. Master.
Kwa	..	For. To. By			European man
Salamu	..	Greetings ! (*when writing*)	Memsaab	..	Madam. European lady
Kwa heri	..	Goodbye !	Sumile	..	Make way !
Ndio[1]	..	Yes. It is so	Hapana (*Siyo*)		No
Hapa	..	Here.	Gani[2]	..	What sort of ?
Habari	..	News			Which ?
Mzuri[2]	..	Good. Excellent	Tu[2]	..	.. Just. Only

In Swahili the syllable ends with a vowel, so letters following it cannot alter its sound, *i.e.*, the above words are syllabilized thus : **Ja-mbo, Sa-la-mu, Ndi-o, Ha-ba-ri, Mzu-ri,** etc. It therefore follows that all true Swahili words will end in a vowel. **Memsaab** is therefore shown to be a word of foreign derivation (actually from Hindustani).

TRANSLATE.—How d'you do, Sir ? How d'you do, Madam ? How d'you do, Murunga ? What's the news here ? Just good news, Sir. Yes, Madam. No, Sir. Goodbye Sir. Goodbye Madam. Make way for the Master.

NOUN CLASSES.

In correct coastal Swahili, nouns are rigidly divided into many classes (generally recognisable by their prefixes) and adjectives pronouns, etc., are varied to agree with them and with their plurals.

In Up-country Swahili this is reduced to a minimum, the form used[3], being almost invariably that which agrees with the singular of the so-called **N-** class.[4]

---

[1]   A confusion may arise over **Ndio** unless it is understood that it means " It is so " rather than " yes "   One may say to a native " he has not yet come ? " and the native may reply " **Ndio Bwana** " meaning correctly, " It is so, Sir (he has not yet come)," whereas in English the " Yes, Sir " would mean that " he has come."

[2]   **Gani** and **Mzuri** follow their noun.   **Gani** is often used to mean " what ? " or " which ? "   **Tu** comes at the end of its phrase.

[3]   When a certain form of speech is said to be, or not to be, " in general use," the words " in up-country districts " are always implied.

[4]   As the Swahili tongue cannot tolerate an **N** before certain other consonants, many of the nouns in the **N-** class do not actually start with **N**.

Learn the following vocabulary, taking sixteen words at a time, write them out in two columns of English and Swahili. After you have read them over several times cover up the English side and translate the Swahili into English, when you can do this cover the Swahili and translate the English words into Swahili. Each sixteen words will thus make one lesson. When starting another lesson run through the words of the previous lesson before starting on the new ones.

SUBSTANTIVES OF THE N- CLASS.

This class of noun is the same for both singular and plural.

e.g. **Nyuki**=Bee or Bees.   **Ndege**=Bird or Birds.

Nyama ..	Animal		**Siku** ..	Day
Siafu ..	Safari Ant		**Deni** ..	Debt
Ndizi[1] ..	Banana		**Fereji** ..	Ditch
Ngambo	Bank, The opposite		**Ngoma** ..	Drum
Nyuki ..	Bee		**Baruti** ..	Explosive
Kengele ..	Bell			
Ndege ..	Bird		**Baba** ..	Father
Damu ..	Blood		**Tupa** ..	File
Ndugu ..	Brother or sister		**Samaki** ..	Fish
Ndoo ..	Bucket		**Nyama** ..	Flesh. Meat
Siagi ..	Butter		**Nguvu** ..	Force. Strength
Ndama ..	Calf		**Rafiki** ..	Friend
Merikani	Calico. Cotton sheeting		**Mbuzi**[1] ..	Goat
Kofia ..	Cap. Hat		**Inchi** ..	Ground. Country
Ngombe	Cattle. Oxen		**Njugu** ..	Ground-nuts
Risasi ..	Cartridge. Lead		**Bunduki** ..	Gun. Rifle
			Nusu ..	Half
Saa ..	Clock. Watch		**Nyundo** ..	Hammer
Nguo ..	Clothing		**Asali** ..	Honey. Treacle
Rungu ..	Club		**Pembe** ..	Horn
Nazi ..	Cocoanut		**Saa** ..	Hour
Kahawa ..	Coffee		**Nyumba** ..	House
Rangi ..	Colour. Paint			
Pamba ..	Cotton. Cotton-wool		**Njaa** ..	Hunger
Pembe ..	Corner. Cob (of Maize)		**Safari** ..	Journey
Ndugu ..	Cousin		**Namna** ..	Kind. Sort
Dasturi ..	Custom		**Ngazi** ..	Ladder
Ngoma ..	Dance		**Taa** ..	Lamp

1 Words starting in **Nd, Ng** or **Mb**, etc., must NOT be pronounced **Nidizi, Nigambo** or **Mibuzi.** If difficulty is experienced in pronouncing these, put a short " I " in front of the N or a short " U " in front of the M, *i.e.*, **Indizi, Ingambo** or **Umbuzi,** then shorten the " I " or " U " until it hardly exists. This faint " I " or " U " sound is why some writers love to put an apostrophe in front of so many African words.

Ngozi	..	Leather	Faida	..	Profit. Gain
Barua	..	Letter	Mali	...	Property
Ndimu	..	Lime (*fruit*)	Robo	..	Quarter
Nzige	..	Locust	Mvua	..	Rain
Hasara	..	Loss	Bara-Bara		Road, main
Ndume	..	Male animal			
Dawa	..	Medicine. Chemicals	Kamba	..	Rope. Strips of bark
Mama	..	Mother	Kondoro		Sheep
Nyumbu		Mule	Ngao	..	Shield
Sindano	..	Needle	Ngozi	..	Skin
			Nyoka	..	Snake
Habari	..	News	Sabuni	..	Soap
Hesabu	..	Number	Nafasi	..	Space. Time
Nafasi	..	Opportunity	Meza	..	Table
Ngombe		Oxen	Chai	..	Tea
Karatasi	..	Paper	Hema	..	Tent
Njia	..	Path. Minor road	Kiu	..	Thirst
Namna	..	Pattern	Nyanya	..	Tomato
Kalamu	..	Pen	Mboga		Vegetables
Nguzo	..	Pillar. Post	Fimbo	..	Walking-stick
Sahani	..	Plate	Nganu	..	Wheat
Sumu	..	Poison	Dawa	..	Witchcraft charms
Nungu	..	Porcupine	Kazi	..	Work

ADJECTIVES.

Correctly, adjectives should agree with their nouns by adopting the same prefix. The following adjectives are correct for the N- class, and are generally used in this form for all other classes.

Bad ..	..	.. Mbaya	Narrow ..	..	Nyembamba
Bitter	..	.. Chungu	New	..	.. Mpya[2]
Black	..	.. Nyeusi	Open	..	.. Wazi
Chief[1]	..	.. Kuu	Raw	..	.. Mbichi
Dark coloured		.. Nyeusi	Red	..	.. Nyekundu
Empty	..	.. Tupu	Rotten ..	..	Mbovu
Fierce	..	.. Kali	Sharp ..	..	Kali
Hard	..	.. Ngumu	Thick ..	..	Nene
How many ?		.. Ngapi	Unripe	..	Mbichi
Light coloured		.. Nyeupe	White ..	..	Nyeupe

Adjectives are always placed after their noun, in the reverse order to that in English. The Articles are omitted.

---

[1] This is generally only found in the phrase **Siku kuu**, meaning Christmas or Birthday.

[2] **Mpya** might be written 'Mpya as it has a faint " um " sound though not strong enough to make it **Umpya**. The accent therefore falls on the 'M.

The following adjectives are generally used in the form given with all classes of noun, *but correctly many of them should have an N- prefix when used with nouns of the* **N-** *Class, e.g., Nzuri Ndogo, Nzito.*[1]

Beautiful ..	**Mzuri**	Idle ..	..	**Mvivu**
Big ..	**Mkubwa**	Long	..	**Mrefu**
Different ..	**Ingine** ·	Many	..	**Mingi** or **Nyingi**
Feminine ..	**Muke** (*Mke*)	Masculine ..		**Mume**
Fine ..	**Mzuri**	Other	..	**Ingine**
Good ..	**Mzuri** (*Mwema*)	Short	..	**Mfupi**
Healthy ..	**Mzima**	Small	..	**Kidogo** or **Mdogo**
Heavy ..	**Mzito**	Whole	..	**Mzima**

Adjectives are few in number and broad in meaning.

e.g., **Mkubwa**=Big, Large, Great, Grand, Main, Chief, etc.

Do the following exercise, writing the English and its translation in two columns as with the vocabulary, then return later, cover up one side and translate until you attain speed and accuracy. The solutions will be found at the end of the book.

TRANSLATE.—A sharp horn. Tough meat. A fierce animal. Unripe bananas. The little bell. Red blood. The white bucket. Good butter. Another brother. Many safari ants. The opposite bank. Bad calico. A beautiful hat. The new clock. Black cattle. A heavy cartridge. Black clothes. A different club. Many cocoanuts. Good coffee. Red paint. White cotton. A large cob (of maize). A female cousin. Different customs. A fine dance. The chief day. Christmas. A large debt. A heavy drum. Black gun-powder. Sharp files. Rotten meat. New force. A male friend. A strict (fierce) father. A slender fish. A vicious goat. Beautiful country. Many ground-nuts. A heavy gun. The other half. The whole hammer. A new calf. Many bees. Dark coloured honey. A large house. What's the time ? (How many hours ?).

Adjectives, as also nouns and verbs, can be intensified by the use of **Sana.**

e.g., **Ndege mkubwa sana** = A very large bird.
      Njaa sana   =· Great hunger.

---

[1] Paragraphs or words in Italics give the more correct coastal forms, which, when met, should be recognised, but which are not normally used up-country, nor in our exercises. See Introduction.

Na = And or With.

TRANSLATE.—A sister in great hunger. A long journey with many losses. What kind of ladder ? (ladder kind what sort of). What lamp ? Hard leather. How many letters ? Very bitter limes. Very many locusts, with many birds. Male cattle. Very bitter medicine. A kind mother. A savage mule. A sharp needle. Good news. A great number. A lazy ox. Thick paper and thin paper. A long narrow path. A hard black pen. The tall post. Beautiful little plates. Strong (fierce) poison. A porcupine with very many quills (needles). What profit ? Little property. Scant opportunity. An open space. A very long road. The whole rope. Hungry sheep. A hard shield. An empty skin. The whole snake. What sort of soap ? Very little time. The small white tables. An empty tent. Great thirst. Unripe tomatoes. An open ditch. Rotten vegetables. Bitter vinegar. A short white walking-stick. Unripe wheat. Very potent (fierce) witchcraft charms. Very much hard work. What sort of pattern ?

Namna Gani=" What sort of pattern " is also used to mean " in what way ? " or even " why ? "

DEMONSTRATIVES.

The demonstratives for the **N-** class are as follows :—

	This = **Hii**	These =*Hizi*
	That = **Ile**	Those =*Zile*
Also		
	Of = **Ya** (*singular*)	Of =*Za* (*plural*)

The plural forms are not often met[1], and the singular forms as for the **N-** class are those generally used with all other classes.

Ile, Zile, and all other forms of the word meaning " that " should only be used of something rather distant, two objects equally near would both be **Hii.**

The order of nouns, adjectives, demonstratives, etc , when joined to each other is the exact reverse of the English order.

These three large black oxen=**Ngombe nyeusi mkubwa tatu hii.**

---

[1] But **Siku Hizi**= " these days." or " nowadays." " lately." is in common use.

NUMBERS.

1	Moja		20	Ishirini
2	Mbili		21	Ishirini na moja
3	Tatu		22	Ishirini na mbili, etc.
4	Ine		30	Thelathini
5	Tano		40	Arobaini
6	Sita		50	Hamsini
7	Saba		60	Sitini
8	Nane		70	Sabaini
9	Tisa		80	Thamanini
10	Kumi		90	Tisini
11	Kumi na moja		100	Mia moja
12	Kumi na Mbili		200	Mia mbili
13	Kumi na tatu, etc.		1000	Elfu moja

Numbers 1, 2, 3, 4, 5, and 8, should, correctly, be variable with other classes of noun, but actually the above forms are generally used for all classes.

2,752 black cartridges=**Risasi nyeusi elfu mbili mia saba hamsini na mbili.**

TRANSLATE —Those four safari ants. Two large caps. What's the time ?[1] Three hours. These five large heavy clubs. This sort. Like this. Those six empty houses. These five long ladders. One lamp. Ten cartridges. Forty letters. Eight pens. Seven sharp needles. Those nine plates. One and a half hours. Twelve tents. Sixteen letters and nine pens. Ninety-three tables. 274 walking-sticks. 581¼ days. twenty-five bananas. Six short rifles and thirty-seven very heavy cartridges. Fifty-four long black posts. 561 hats. 12,687 rotten tomatoes and 34,721 unripe bananas.

A form of the verb " To Be " is introduced by putting the demonstrative before the adjective.

This large ox = **Ngombe mkubwa hii**
This ox is large = **Ngombe hii mkubwa**

In other cases, the present tense of the verb " To Be," as used in English, may be merely omitted in Swahili.

Red paint is poison = **Rangi nyekundu sumu**

TRANSLATE.—This white paper is heavy. That medicine is bitter. That wheat is unripe. These ten buckets are white. This leather is very hard. This tea is very strong (fierce). This work is very bad. This very big rope is very heavy. Snakes are very numerous nowadays.

---

[1] For " telling the time " see p. 41.

NOUNS OF THE M- CLASSES.

Many Nouns which Denote Living Beings commence with
M- and make their plural by changing the M- into Wa-.

Mutu[1] (*Mtu*)	= A person	Watu	= People
Mtoto	= A child	Watoto	= Children
Mwana Mume[2]	= A male. Man	Wana Waume[3]	= Males
Mwana Muke[2]	= A female. Woman	Wana Wake	= Females. Women
Mzee	= An old person	Wazee	= Old people

Other similar nouns are :—

Mzungu	= A European	Mgeni	= A stranger
Mgonjwa	= A sick man	Mjinga	= A fool
Mchungi	= A herdsman	Mshenzi	= An uncivilised man

Adjectives with this class should have the same prefix as the
noun, and this also applies to the variable numerals 2, 3, 4, 5, and 8,
which become **Wawili, Watatu, Wanne, Watano** and **Wanane.**

Watu warefu wawili = Two tall men

But owing to elision we have :—

Watu weusi = Black people   Watu wengi = Many people
Watu wengine = Other people

Demonstratives are :—

This = **Huyu**   These = **Hawa**
That = *Yule*   Those = **Wale**

Also   Of = **Wa** for both singular and plural.

The above, with perhaps the exception of **Yule,** are often
heard correctly used, though also the adjectives and demonstratives of the N- class are heard, possibly even more often.

Translate using the correct form.—This man. Three idle
old men. Five tall Europeans. Two men and one woman.
A very old man. A fearful fool. These strangers. These are
strangers. These little old women are very black. This man
is tall, those are short. The house of the European. The child
of the European. The sick man's medicine. These herdsmen
are fools. These savages' clothes are black. The savages are black.

---

[1] Correctly **'Mtu,** but up-country there seems to be a reluctance to
put the accent on **'M,** and it is therefore often changed to **Mu** when it
is the accentuated syllable. *E.g.*, **'Mto** = pillow, becomes **Muto.**
'Mti = tree, takes its plural form and becomes **Miti.** **'Mpa** = give him,
becomes **Mupa,** etc., though **'Mpya** = new, retains its correct form,
with the accent on the **'M.**

[2] The words " Man " and " Woman " normally would both be
translated as " **Mutu,**" unless their sex is to be stressed.

[3] Often contracted to **wanaume.**

NOUNS OF THE **M-** CLASS WHICH DO NOT DENOTE LIVING BEINGS *make their plural by changing* **M-** *into* **Mi-** *their adjectives and the variable numerals doing likewise.*

The Demonstratives are :—

This = *Huu*	These = **Hii**
That = *Ule*	Those = **Ile**

Also

Of = **Wa** (*singular*) and **Ya** (*plural*)

Actually with this class, as with some others of the previous class, one form is generally used for both singular and plural, and adjectives, demonstratives, etc., are used in the form correct for the **N-** Class. The following are nouns of both types of **M-** class in the form generally used for both singular and plural.

Milima	..	Ant-hills	Mwezi	..	Month
Mikono	..	Arms. Hands	Mwezi	..	Moon
Mwanzo	..	Beginning	Milima	..	Mountains
Mwili	..	Body	Mwenyewe		Owner
Mifupa	..	Bones	Muto (*Mto*)		Pillow
Mpaka	..	Boundary	Miti	..	Poles
Mizigo	..	Bundles	Mtoni (*Mto*)		River
Mtumbwi	..	Canoe			
Mwenzi	..	Companion	Moshi	..	Smoke
Mpishi	..	Cook	Mikuke	..	Spears
Mizabibu	..	Currants	Mwiko	..	Spoon (*large*
Milango	..	Doors			*wooden*), Spade
Mulevi	..	Drunkard	Miti	..	Sticks
Mwisho	..	End	Mkia	..	Tail
Moto	..	Fire	Mwalimu	..	Teacher
Miguu	..	Feet	Mwivi	..	Thief
			Mwiba	..	Thorn
Mchezo	..	Game, A	Mikebe	..	Tins (*small*)
Mungu	..	God	Mitego	..	Traps
Mikono	..	Hands	Miti	..	Trees
Moyo	..	Heart	Mlingoti	..	Wagon-pole
Miguu	..	Legs	Mtungi	..	Water-jar
Midomo	..	Lips	Msharidi	..	Whip
Mizigo	..	Loads	Muchawi	..	Witch-doctor
Mkate	..	Loaf of bread	Mwaka	..	Year
Mlingoti	..	Mast			

TRANSLATE.—This ant-hill is high. Two arms. One hand. A bad beginning. The whole body. A hard bone. These bundles are very heavy. Two large canoes. This cook is very lazy. The companion of the teacher is a drunkard. Many currants. These thick doors. This man's foot. The child's game. These are the herdsman's spears, the cook is the owner of this spear. God's affair (Shauri). The heart of an ox. Two red lips. The cook's bread is very bad. This tall mast. Those high mountains. The moon is red. Four white pillows. This boundary is the river. The sick man's leg. A tall master. The witch doctor's medicine. The black man's spoons. An animal's tail. These are the European's traps. A month of thirty days. Two European ladies. The opposite bank of the river. The beginning of the trees. These are different water jars. The end of the year. The people of the trees. The smoke of the fire is very dark. A cattle thief. The body of a girl child. A slender thorn. A wagon-pole of strength. Twenty empty tins. A strong whip.

PERSONAL PRONOUNS.

The full forms of these are as follows :—

I	= **Mimi**	We	= *Sisi*
You	= **Wewe**	You	= *Ninyi*
He or she	= **Yeye**	They (*people*)	= *Wao*

The plural pronouns are not often heard, except occasionally **Ninyi** when the plural meaning is to be stressed.

In the actual presence of the third person or persons it is more common to use the demonstratives.

He or She = **Huyu**   They = **Hawa**

For inanimate objects the demonstrative is always used.

It or They (Things) = **Hii** (if near) or **Ile** (if distant)

Self = **Mwenyewe**   I myself = **Mimi mwenyewe**

INTERROGATIVES.

Who ?	= **Nani ?**	When ?	= *Lini* ?
What ?	= **Nini ?**	How many ?	= **Ngapi ?**[1]
Where ?	= **Wapi ?**	Of what sort ?	= **Gani ?**[1]

Lini is not very generally understood, **Siku gani** = Which day ? or **Saa ngapi** = What hour ? adequately fill the gap. **Gani** also usurps the correct word for " which ? "

---

[1] **Ngapi** and **Gani,** being equivalent to adjectives, follow the noun.

TRANSLATE.—Who are you ? Where are the men ? How many of them ? Who is this old man ? We are strangers. I am a European. They are black men. What is this ? What sort of a tree is this ? Which tree ? I myself am sick. They are witch-doctors. He is the teacher. Who is the child ? He is the child of whom ? Where is the house of the owner of these cattle ? He is old. He is sick. What sort of illness ? Illness of the foot. Which foot ? You are a fool.

THE VERB.

The verb is conjugated by the use of personal prefixes followed by tense prefixes.

The personal prefixes are :—

I	=	Ni-	We	=	Tu-
You	=	U-	You (plural)	=	M-
He or she	=	A-	They	=	Wa-

The prefixes for It and They (of things) *vary with the different classes of nouns in correct Swahili, the form being always the same as the second syllable of the correct word for "This" (i.e., for* N-*class* I- *(sing.)* Zi- *(Plu.) etc.).* Actually the form I- is the one almost always used, as for the singular of the N- class.

The second person plural is seldom heard.

Some of the commonest tense prefixes are :—

Ku- for the Infinitive.

-me- for the Present Perfect. -ta- for the Future

Kupiga = To beat or strike.

Nimepiga	= I have beaten	**Nitapiga**	= I shall beat
Umepiga	= You have beaten	**Utapiga**	= You will beat
Amepiga	= He has beaten	**Atapiga**	= He will beat
Tumepiga	= We have beaten	**Tutapiga**	= We will beat
Wamepiga	= They have beaten	**Watapiga**	= They will beat

Imepiga = It or they (of things) has or have struck.
Itapiga = It or they (of things) will strike.

The interrogative is expressed merely by the tone of the voice.

Kupiga also has many other different meanings in connection with different nouns.

B

Ngoma	= A drum	Kupiga Ngoma	= To beat the drum, or to have a dance
Kengele	= A bell	Kupiga Kengele	= To ring a bell
Bunduki	= A gun or rifle	Kupiga Bunduki	= To shoot
Simu	= Telegraph	Kupiga Simu	= To telegraph
Pasi	= A clothes-iron	Kupiga Pasi	= To iron clothes
Hodi	= May I come in ?	Kupiga Hodi	= To knock at a door
Kelele	= A noise	Kupiga Kelele	= To make a noise
Randa	= A carpenter's plane	Kupiga Randa	= To plane wood
Pampa	= A pump	Kupiga Pampa	= To pump
Mvua	= Rain	Mvua Kupiga	= To rain
Hema	= A tent	Kupiga Hema	= To pitch or to strike a tent
Laini (Mstari)	= A line	Kupiga Laini	= To draw a line
Firimbi	= A whistle	Kupiga Firimbi	= To blow a whistle

Also there are the following, which are not often heard up-country :—

Kupiga Teke	= *To kick*	*Kupiga Chapa*	= *To print*
Kupiga Mbio	= *To run*	*Kupiga Makofi*	= *To clap the hands*

And *others besides, still less often heard.*

TRANSLATE.—I have rung the bell. You will fire the gun. He will work the pump. Where shall we pitch the tent ? He has ironed the clothes. They will make a great outcry (be very angry). Have you knocked at the door ? It will rain. I have planed the doors. They will telegraph. Where have you drawn the line ? He will whistle.

Two other tense prefixes are :—

  Na- for the Present Imperfect. **Li-** for the Pluperfect.

Ninapiga	= *I am striking*	**Nilipiga**	= I struck
Unapiga	= *You are striking*	**Ulipiga**	= You struck
Anapiga	= He is striking	**Alipiga**	= He struck
Tunapiga	= *We are striking*	**Tulipiga**	= We struck
Wanapiga	= They are striking	**Walipiga**	= They struck

  Inapiga[1] = It or They (of things) is or are striking

  Ilipiga = It or They (of things) struck

---

[1] The personal prefix of **Inapiga**, and of the same tense of all other verbs, is often dropped, leaving **Napiga** to mean " it strikes." In fact, in more debased Swahili the form **Napiga** is used for all persons and all tenses of the verb.

The three persons shown on the preceding page in Italics are not very often heard, their place more usually being taken by the following :—

[1] **Napiga**　=　I strike　　　**Twapiga**　=　We strike
Wapiga　=　You strike

Also, instead of **Nilipiga** the form **Nalipiga** is generally used.

[2] The IMPERATIVE, in the singular, consists of the verb root by itself, and in the plural, of the verb root, with the termination **ni** added.

Piga ! = Strike !　　　**Pigani !** = Strike (all of you) !

Often in correct Swahili the final **-a** is changed to **-e**, but **Lete !** = Bring ! is the only case of this that is in general use.

TRANSLATE.—We struck the door with a hammer. Strike hard ! We are ironing the clothes. Whom did you strike ? He struck me. I am ringing a bell. They struck the drum. We are having a dance. I fired the gun. Ring the bell ! They are beating the oxen. She beat the child. I knocked at the door. We are making a great noise. Iron these clothes. It struck the house. You ironed these clothes very badly. Bring two plates.

When a noun is the subject, the appropriate personal prefix is still used.

TRANSLATE.—The teacher planed the door. The old man and I made a great noise. The herdsman and the child have beaten the oxen. Will it rain ? The child is hitting the goat. The hammer hit the gunpowder. Rain is falling hard. The cook is beating the witch-doctor. They have shot the animals. I am hitting the drunkard with a stick. This old man and I have beaten the ground-nuts with clubs.

---

[1] The complete present Indefinite Tense actually exists with -a- as its tense prefix, but elision takes place with the vowel of the personal prefix to form combined prefixes as follows :—**Na- Wa- A- Twa- Mwa- Wa.**

[2] *There are many other tenses, such as, Nikipiga = In the event of my hitting. Nikapiga = And I hit. Ningalipiga = I should have hit, etc. but these are not generally understood or used by up ·country natives.*

VERBS.

Learn this vocabulary, sixteen words at a time.

Kuweza	..	To be Able	Kuangalia	..	To take Care
„ kubali	..	„ Accept	„ chukua	..	„ Carry
„ sumbua		„ Annoy	„ kamata	..	„ Catch hold of
„ onekana		„ Appear	„ danganya		„ Cheat
„ fika	..	„ Arrive	„ dai	..	„ Claim a debt from
„ omba	..	„ Ask for			
„ amuka	..	„ Awake	„ safisha	..	„ Clean
„ oga	..	„ Bathe	„ panda	..	„ Climb
„ zaa	..	„ Bear fruit	„ rudi	..	„ Come back
„ chemuka		„ Boil. Bubble	„ toka	..	„ Come from
„ kopa	..	„ Borrow	„ shinda	..	„ Conquer
„ leta	..	„ Bring	„ fikiri	..	„ Consider
„ jenga	..	„ Build	„ pika	..	„ Cook
„ choma	..	„ Burn. Set on fire	„ kohoa	..	„ Cough
			„ funika	..	„ Cover up
„ ungua	..	„ Burn. Catch fire	„ lia	..	„ Cry
„ nunua	..	„ Buy	„ lima	..	„ Cultivate

The poverty of the Swahili vocabulary results in one word covering many shades of meaning, our exercises are therefore partly training in twisting normal English to conform to the words available.

TRANSLATE.—I can cook. We accept. She will annoy the cook. The locusts have appeared. The teacher will arrive. Ask for a lamp. I shall wake up. He bathed in the river. This tree will bear fruit. The woman has had a baby. The vegetables are boiling. The medicine is bubbling. He borrowed a hat. Bring six plates. I will build a new house. I am burning this paper. The house is burning. You have bought twenty oxen. Look out ! Carry these loads. He caught hold of the ox's tail. This one is a thief, he cheated the cook and now (sasa) he claims a debt from me. Take care to clean the gun thoroughly. Climb up that pillar. You have come back. Where do you come from ? I have considered the matter (shauri). The work defeats me. The cook cooks. The sick man coughs. Cover up the butter. They are crying hard. Have you cultivated the bananas ?

The objective personal prefix, in correct Swahili, is as follows, and is inserted after the tense prefix.

Me ..	..	-ni-	Us ..	..	-tu-
You ..	..	-ku-	You ..	..	-wa-
Him or her ..		-m-	Them	..	-wa-

Thus

He will hit me ..	**Atanipiga**	He will hit us ..	**Atatupiga**
He will hit you ..	**Atakupiga**	He will hit you ..	**Atawapiga**
He will hit her ..	**Atampiga**	He will hit them ..	**Atawapiga**

These objective prefixes are generally used correctly with the following verbs.

Kuuliza ..	To Ask a question	**Kuua** ..	To Kill
„ **uma** ..	„ Bite or Sting	„ **jua** ..	„ Know
„ **ita** ..	„ Call	„ **umiza** ..	„ Pain
„ **ona** ..	„ Find or See	„ **onyesha**	„ Show
„ **pa** ..	„ Give	„ **ambia** ..	„ Tell

Before a vowel the **M-** of the third person singular becomes **Mw-**.

Nitamwambia = I shall tell him.

TRANSLATE.—I will ask him where is the child. Tell (him) this (man) to call me. Call him ! The bee has stung me. I shall see them. He found you. Give me the cow's horn. Give it to him. I will give them medicine. She has killed him. I know him. They will know me. This foot is hurting me badly. This man will show the cook (how) to cook the bread. Will you tell him ? No, I will tell him myself. They have told me.

The following table summarises the verb tenses and prefixes and is useful for practice in their rapid selection.

SUBJECT		TENSE		OBJECT		VERB	
I ..	.. **Ni**	Did ..	.. **Li**	Me ..	.. **Ni**	Hit ..	**Piga**
You (s)	.. **U**	Has, Have ..	**Me**	You (s)	.. **Ku**		
He or She ..	**A**	Am, Are, Is	**Na**	Him or Her	**M**		
We ..	.. **Tu**	Do, Does ..	**A**	Us ..	.. **Tu**		
You (pl)	.. **M**	Will ..	.. **Ta**	You (pl)	.. **Wa**		
They ..	.. **Wa**			Them..	.. **Wa**		
It or They ..	**I**						

He struck me = He did me hit .. **Alinipiga**

I strike him = I do him hit .. **N'ampiga**

Using this chart do the following exercises verbally, as fast as possible, then do it several times without the chart until you achieve rapidity.

TRANSLATE.—I am hitting you. You (pl) strike us. They will hit them. He has hit him. We struck you (pl). You (s) strike me. We are hitting them. It has hit me. They (things) will hit you (s). You have hit us. They (men) are hitting us. I struck you (s). We will hit him. He struck her. She is hitting him. It hits me. They (men) struck you (s). I have hit them. You (s) will hit us.

The above is the correct way to use the personal prefixes in all cases, but with verbs other than those just given the objective prefixes are not often used correctly up-country, where the more usual form of speech consists in introducing the full form of the personal pronoun for the object, and often, by way of emphasis, for the subject also.

I strike you = **Mimi napiga wewe.**
He struck me = **Huyu alipiga mimi.**

A still more debased form very often used is to ignore all tense and personal prefixes and use the **Napiga** form for all present and future tenses, introducing in front of the root of the verb the word **Nakwisha** = I finish, to indicate any past tense.

Huyu nakwisha piga mimi = He struck me.

As natives will very largely take the standard of their Swahili from that of their masters, our exercises will deal with the less debased form, a proper knowledge of which will lead to avoidance of many misunderstandings.

The verb **Kwisha** may often correctly be used with another verb to emphasise that the action is completed.

Nimekwisha safisha sahani = I have already cleaned the plates.
Amekwisha kufa = He is quite dead.

Learn this vocabulary.

Kupona ..	To become Cured	**Kupigana**	To Fight
„ **chelewa**	„ Delay	„ **maliza**	„ Finish
„ **teremuka**	„ Descend	„ **kunja** ..	„ Fold
„ **chimba**	„ Dig	„ **fuata** ..	„ Follow
„ **fanya** ..	„ Do	„ **sahau** ..	„ Forget
„ **buruta** ..	„ Drag away	„ **shiba** ..	„ be Full with food
„ **fukuza** ..	„ Drive away	„ **pata** ..	„ Get
„ **lewa** ..	„ get Drunk	„ **toka** ..	„ Get out
„ **kauka** ..	„ become Dry	„ **toa** ..	„ Give out
„ **anika** ..	„ put out to Dry	„ **rudi** ..	„ Go back
„ **ingia** ..	„ Enter	„ **oza** ..	„ Go bad
„ **kosa** ..	„ Fail	„ **tangulia**	„ Go before
„ **anguka** ..	„ Fall	„ **saga** ..	„ Grind
„ **nona** ..	„ get Fat	„ **sikia** ..	„ Hear
„ **funga** ..	„ Fasten	„ **saidia** ..	„ Help
„ **ogopa** ..	„ Fear	„ **ficha** ..	„ Hide

[1]TRANSLATE.—The sick man has become cured. He delayed to enter the house. We will descend the hill. Dig a ditch. What are you doing ? Many trees have fallen down, drag them away with oxen. Put out these clothes to dry. They are dry already. You have made a mistake. You are getting very fat. I am afraid of snakes, fasten the door. I struck him and he fought with me. I will finish this bread and I shall be full. I told you to fold the clothes in this manner, have you forgotten ? The cook is drunk, send him away, I shall get another, have you told him to get out of the house ? I will give out wheat for the mule. I shall return. The butter is rancid. Walk in front of me. Did you hear me grinding the cocoanut ? We will help him to hide the other lamp.

Single syllable verbs, or those of which the root starts with a vowel, keep the prefix **Ku** for euphony in many of their tenses. The following are those verbs with which this is usually done.

Kuwa	..	To Be or Become	**Kula**	..	To Eat
„ **anza**	..	„ Begin	„ **isha**	..	„ End
„ **ja**	..	„ Come	„ **isha**	..	„ be Finished
„ **fa**	..	„ Die	„ **enda**	..	„ Go

The verb **Kupa** = To Give, does not come into this category, as it is always used with an objective prefix which displaces the **Ku-**.

The **Ku-** becomes **Kw-** before vowels a, e & i, hence **Kwanza, Kwisha** and **Kwenda.**

The imperative of **Kuja** is irregular.

Njoo = Come !   Njooni = Come ye

The verb **Kuwa** = To Be is not used in the present tense.

TRANSLATE.—I shall be ill. He was a fool. You will begin at the beginning and you will finish at the end. I will finish up the honey and the honey will be finished. The sick man is quite dead. Come ! We will begin work. They ate the bread. Master the butter is finished, the child has eaten it. I shall go to the house, will you come ? Go away ! Get out ! Come ! (all of you).

---

[1] It is impossible to lay down definitely when the full form of the Personal Pronoun should be used, but the tendency is to use it more frequently than is really necessary for emphasis.

POSSESSIVE PRONOUNS.

Those in general use are as for the N- class nouns.

My	..	..	**Yangu**	Our	..	..	**Yetu**
Thy	..	..	**Yako**	Your (*plural*)	..	**Yenu**
His or her	..	**Yake**	Their	..	..	**Yao**
It's	..	..	**Yake**	All	..	,.	**Yote**

Correctly the **Y-** *should be changed to* **W-,** *making* **wangu, Wako,**
etc., with the singular of both **M-** *classes,* but actually these forms
are rarely met, except with the **Watu** class of plurals (see p. 14).

Wazee wangu wote = All my old people.
Watoto wako = Your children.

VOCABULARY.

Learn the following conjunctions, etc.

Halafu	Afterwards. And then	**Au ... Au** ..	Either . . . Or
Tena ..	Again. Also	**Labda** ..	Perhaps
Lakini	But	**Kisha** ..	Then. When that's
Mpaka	As far as		finished
Kama	If. As	**Hata** ..	Until. Even
Ni Heri	It is advisable to	**Hata Kidogo**	Not even a little
Lazma	It is necessary to	**Kama** ..	When
Sasa ..	Now	**Kwamba** ..	Whether. How that

Ya = Of, is sometimes used before the infinitive of a verb
when " in order to " is understood[1].

-je is sometimes added to a verb to make it a question[2].

Come and help me	= **Njoo ya kunisaidia.**
Go and look for it	= **Kwenda ya kutafuta.**
What are you doing ?	= **Wafanyaje ?**[2]
Where are you going ?	= **Wakwendaje ?**[2]

---

[1] There is an applied form of verb which should be used when a
preposition is omitted. It is seldom used up-country, except sometimes
with this use of **Ya.** It consists of inserting an **-i-** or **-e-** before the
final **-a** of the verb, it being **-i-** when the preceding vowel is " A,"
" I " or " U," and **-e-** when it is " E " or " O."

e.g. **Kupima** = to measure. **Kutoka** = to go out, the applied
forms are **Kupimia** and **Kutokea.** Thus :—

A tin to measure the wheat = **Mikebe ya kupimia ngano.**
A door to go out by = **Milango ya kutokea.**
A stick to beat the cow = **Miti ya kupigia ngombe.**

When the simple verb ends in two vowels an **L** is inserted for
euphony, thus :—

Kusikia = to hear. **Ya kusikilia** = in order to hear.

[2] **Wafanyaje** is the only example of this commonly heard,

Learn this vocabulary.

Kuzuia[1]	To Hinder	Kukutana[3]	To Meet
„ shika	„ Hold	„ shinda	„ Overcome
„ ongeza	„ Increase	„ pita	„ Pass
„ ruka	„ Jump. Fly	„ lipa	„ Pay
„ chinja	„ Kill for food	„ lokota[4]	„ Pick up
„ chelewa	„ be Late	„ weka	„ Place
„ wacha[2]	„ Leave	„ vuta	„ Pull
„ inua	„ Lift up	„ sukuma	„ Push
„ penda	„ Like	„ tia	„ Put
„ sikiliza	„ Listen	„ tandika	„ Put on the accessories
„ tazama	„ Look		
„ angalia	„ Look at carefully	„ weka	„ Put away
		„ tengeneza	„ Put to rights
„ tafuta	„ Look for	„ gombana	„ Quarrel
„ legeza	„ Loosen	„ soma	„ Read
„ fanya	„ Make	„ tengeneza	„ get a thing Ready
„ pima	„ Measure		
		„ kataa	„ Refuse

TRANSLATE.—Either the old man, or his companion, or both, (all two) have prevented the cook from quarrelling with the child. The child holds the rope of the oxen, we call him the **Mshika-kamba**. I can increase the number of our cattle if you will help me. All your goats have jumped the river, do you hear ? Bring me my gun, I am going out to kill an animal (for food). You are late again, perhaps you are ill ? Now what are you doing ? Just leave it alone ! Raise the lamp, I am looking for some soap. If you listen hard perhaps you will hear an animal. What are you looking at ? Look very carefully at these bones, give me others of this sort if you find them. Go, look for the cattle as far as the river, then return to tell me whether you have found them. I like bananas very much. Loosen this rope again as far as its end. Have you done all your work ? Make room for twelve plates. I will weigh this wheat if you will measure this ladder. I met thirty-two men, but when they saw me they hid, but I called them and then they came. When I passed the children they were jumping. I will pay all the men

---

[1] **Kusibia** is often heard instead of **kuzuia**.

[2] The correct form is **Ku-acha,** but **Kuwacha** is the form normally used.

[3] This is the reciprocal form of **Kukuta,** the -a changes to -ana to indicate the " one another " idea.
Kupiga = To beat. **Kupigana** = To beat one another = To fight.

[4] The correct form is **Ku-okota,** but **Kulokota** is the form often heard.

later. It is necessary to pick up this file. Where have you placed the lamp ? Perhaps those white oxen will pull well. Come and push the motor-car[1] everybody, push hard, push with force ! Put the plates here now, then when I have finished eating, put them away. Saddle my mule ! Have you laid the table ? I will examine the lamp and put it right, then I will get my gun ready. The cook is quarrelling dreadfully with his child. The fool refuses to read. It is advisable to take care when you descend a steep hill.

VERBS ARE MADE PASSIVE by inserting a **-w-** before the final vowel.

Kupiga	= To beat	**Kupigwa**	= To be beaten
Kukata	= To cut	**Kukatwa**	= To be cut
Kutumia	= To use	**Kutumiwa**	= To be used

For euphony the passive termination sometimes becomes **-iwa** or **-ewa**, or when a vowel precedes the final **-a**, by **-liwa** or **-lewa**. Of this type the following verbs are among the commonest in general use.

Kuzaa ..	To Give birth	**Kuzaliwa** ..	To be	Born
„ **lima** ..	„ Cultivate	„ **limiwa** ..	„ „	Cultivated
„ **oa** ..	„ Marry a wife	„ **olewa** ..	„ „	Married to a husband
„ **pima** ..	„ Measure	„ **pimiwa**	„ „	Measured or weighed
„ **choma**	„ Burn	„ **chomiwa**	„ „	Burnt (intentionally)

There is also a NEUTER FORM OF VERB, not unlike the passive, which is formed by changing the final **-a** into **-ka,** or for euphony into **-ika.** The following are the commonest of this type in general use.

Kutoboa ..	To Bore a hole in	**Kutoboka** ..	To have a hole in it	
„ **vunja** ..	„ Break	„ **vunjika** ..	„ Be Broken	
„ **haribu**	„ Destroy	„ **haribika**[2]	„ „	Destroyed or Spoilt
„ **mwaga**	„ Empty out	„ **mwagika**	„ „	Emptied out or spilt
, **pindua**	„ Upset	„ **pinduka**	„ become overturned	
„ **pasua**	„ Split something	„ **pasuka** ..	„ become split	

---

[1] As in English. Would be spelt **motokaa.**
[2] **Kuharibika** is often used of machinery to mean merely " out of action."

There is also **Kukata** and **Kukatika,** but in this case **Kukatika** seems more to have a meaning of being broken than of being cut, for which the normal passive form of **Kukatwa** is more often used.

By after a passive verb is translated by **Na.**

TRANSLATE.—The child was beaten by the cook. The cords of the European's bundles were cut by the stranger and his companion. Your water-jar has been upset by this fool, and now it has a hole in it. He was married afterwards. She will be married again. The honey is all spoilt, the child overturned the bucket and spilt the honey. What? Yes, the bucket was overturned and the honey was all spilt. The old man will be called when the ground nuts have been weighed. The child fell, and the plates were all broken. This child is very bad, he has broken the plates again. The door has been fastened. When will the woman give birth? Sir, the child is already born. The plough (**jembe**) is out of action, its wheel (leg) is broken, and it has overturned. It is necessary to burn the skins of these tomatoes, and has that paper been burnt?

VOCABULARY.

Here	..	**Hapa**	Why?	**Kwa Ninj**
There ..	..	**Huko**	Because	**Sababu**
A time ..	..	**Mara**	Every	**Kila**[1]
At once ..	..	**Mara Moja**	Absolutely ..	**Kabisa**
Often	..	**Mara Nyingi**	In, at, to, etc. ..	**Katika**[2]
Twice	..	**Mara Mbili**	By means of ..	**Kwa**
Water	..	**Maji**	To (of a person) ..	**Kwa**

There is a CAUSATIVE FORM OF VERB made by changing the final **-a** or **-ka** into **-za** or **-sha** with occasionally slight alteration for euphony.

Kuamuka ..	To Awaken	**Kuamusha** ..	To Cause to awaken
„ **chemuka**	„ Boil	„ **chemusha**	„ Cause to boil
„ **kopa**	„ Borrow	„ **kopesha**	„ Lend
„ **waka** ..	„ Burn, be on fire	„ **washa** ..	„ Light. Set on fire
„ **rudi** ..	„ Come back	„ **rudisha** ..	„ Send back. Give back

[1] **Kila** is an exception in that it precedes its noun.

[2] **Katika** is an exception in that the accent is on the first syllable. **Kwa** is often used in place of the more correct **Katika.**

Kujaa	..	To become Full	Kujaza	..	To make Full. Fill
„ sikia	..	„ Hear	„ sikiliza	..	„ Listen
„ uma	..	„ Pain. Ache	„ umiza	..	„ Cause to be in pain. Hurt
„ cheka	..	„ Laugh	„ cheza	..	„ Play
„ penda	..	„ Like. Love	„ pendeza		„ Please
„ potea	..	„ become Lost	„ poteza	..	„ Lose
„ kumbuka		„ Remember	„ kumbusha		„ Remind
„ ona	..	„ See	„ onyesha		„ Show
„ simama		„ Stand. Halt	„ simamisha		„ Cause to stand

TRANSLATE.—If you call him once more (another time) he will wake up at once. Go and boil the water. But Master, the water has already boiled. Come back here. Give back my watch. But if I lend it you now, you will borrow it again. Light the fire and come and tell me when it is burning well. This bucket is full, empty it out and fill it once more. But Master, I am very ill, all my body hurts me. I must put some antiseptic on your leg, but I shall hurt you. If I play with him he will laugh often. I like butter, honey pleases me also. Did you lose my letter ? No Master, not me, but it is just lost. If you remind me twice I shall remember. If you show this man he will see and he will know another day. Stand here yourself, and stand this stick up. Now listen, go over there and halt, do you hear ?

NEGATIVES.

Correctly	*Hakuna*	means	*There is none*
	Siyo	„	No
	Hapana	„	*There is none there*
	Bado	„	Not yet

Actually Hakuna and Siyo are seldom heard up-country.

Hapana is used to mean No, and with **Bado**, expresses the negative in all its forms.

Correctly verbs should have their negative tenses formed with the following negative personal prefixes.

Si-	I . . not		Hatu-	We . . not
Hu-	*You . . not*		Ham-	*You . . not*
Ha-	He or she . . not		Hawa-	They . . not
	Hai-	It or they (inanimate) . . not[1]		

---

[1] *Correctly the negative prefix for " It " or " They (of things) " is the same, for each class of noun, as the positive prefix with* Ha- *in front. Thus* Hai-, Hazi-, Hau-, *etc.* But actually only **Hai-** is normally met.

The negative present is formed by the above prefixes with the verb root, but with the final -a of it changed to -i.

The negative future is formed by the above prefixes with the tense prefix -ta-.

The negative past is formed by the above prefixes with the tense prefix -ku-.

Sijui ..	I do not know	**Hajui** ..	He does not know
Sitajua	*I shall not know*	*Hatajua*	*He will not know*
Sikujua	I did not know	**Hakujua**	He did not know

The negative imperative takes the form :—

    L'sijua .. *You are not to know*[1].

The above negative forms should be understood, as they are sometimes met, though (unfortunately) one more often hears the more debased form :—

Mimi hapana piga wewe = I do not (or will not, or have not) hit you.

The following forms are however in almost universal use.

Sijui	..	I do not know.
Sitaki	..	I do not want.
Sipendi	..	I do not like.
Siwezi	..	I am not able. I can't. (By itself may mean "I am ill.")
Hawezi	..	He or she can not. (By itself may mean "He is ill.")
Hataki	..	He or she does not want.
Haithuru !		It does not matter ! (From **Kuthuru** = to injure.)
Haifai !	..	This won't do ! (From **Kufaa** = to be useful.)

To generalise, one might say that the first and third persons singular are the only ones with which the correct negative forms are used up-country.

Learn this vocabulary.

Kufurai	..	To Rejoice	**Kutoroka**	To Run away[4]
„ **baki**	..	„ Remain over[2]	„ **sema**..	„ Say
„ **pumzika**		„ Rest	„ **uza** ..	„ Sell
„ **panda** ..		„ Ride	„ **peleka**[5]	„ Send[5]
„ **iva**	..	„ become Ripe	„ **shona**	„ Sew
„ **oza**	..	„ become Rotten ..	„ **funga**	„ Shut
„ **sugua** ..		„ Rub	„ **chunga**	„ Sift
„ **kimbia**		„ Run[3]	„ **kosa** ..	„ Sin

---

[1] *There are many other negative tenses, but except for "Sijafanya, I have not yet done" they are rarely met up-country.*

[2] Sometimes **Kupakia** is heard.

[3] and [4] *Correctly, to run is Kupiga Mbio, and Kukimbia is to run away.*

[5] The accent is on the first syllable of **Peleka**, but it is not quite as short as **Pelka** would be.

Kuketi	..	To Sit	Kufunga	To Tie
„ lala	..	„ Sleep	„ kaza ..	„ Tighten
„ nuka	..	„ be Smelly	„ choka	„ become Tired
„ kaa	..	„ Stay. To dwell	„ jaribu	„ Try
„ tosha	..	„ Suffice. Be enough	„ fungua	„ Unfasten
„ fagia	..	„ Sweep	„ tumia	„ Use
„ vimba	..	„ become Swollen	„ faa	„ be Useful, suitable
„ ondoa	..	„ Take away	„ ngoja	„ Wait
„ toa	..	„ Take off	„ tembea	„ Walk. Go for a Walk
„ chukua		„ Take up		
„ fundisha		„ Teach	„ taka ..	„ Want
„ chunga		„ Tend, look after	„ nawa	„ Wash the hands
„ konda	..	„ become Thin	„ fua ..	„ Wash clothes
„ fikiri	..	„ Think (deliberate)	„ poteza	„ Waste
			„ vaa ..	„ Wear clothes
„ thani[1]	..	„ Think (suppose)	„ nyima	„ Withhold
„ tupa	..	„ Throw	„ andika	„ Write

TRANSLATE, using the correct negative forms.—Do not refuse. We shall not rejoice. Why did you not rest ? They are not riding. We did not rub hard enough (to suffice). You will not run fast. They have not all run away. These (men) have all run away.

TRANSLATE, using the correct negative forms for the first and third persons singular, but the debased form for the other persons. —Vegetables do not remain, not even a little. I did not say to do it like that. I will not send the clothes, they are not sewn, not yet. Why have you not shut the door ? I was at fault, Master. I do not want to tell you every day. I forgot Master. Do not forget, I can not sleep with an open door. I shall not stay here because the meat smells. You have not swept here enough. She can not sleep, and her leg is very swollen. Tell her to sit down and I will examine it. Take this bucket and put it over there, then come back here and take the skin off these tomatoes. Take away the skins and throw them away. I think that you are wrong, but I will think it over and tell you later, I do not like to be wrong. They will teach the children to throw. Tie this rope and make it very tight. I am not yet tired, I will try again to undo my lamp with force. But this wont do, you are doing it with very little force. It does not matter, I do not want to wait, I will leave it because I want to go for a walk.

---

[1] Sometimes Zani, Thania or Zania.

I have asked my companion to send my cattle to this man, but he refuses, he withholds them, and they are getting exceedingly thin. I will write another letter. But master this work is very hard, I am absolutely tired out.

SUBSTANTIVES OF THE Ki-, Vi- CLASS.

This class of noun has its singular starting with **Ki-** and makes its plural by changing the **Ki-** into **Vi-**. In those nouns of this class which have a vowel following the prefix, this becomes **Ch-** and **Vy-** in place of **Ki-** and **Vi-**.

Kitu	= A Thing	**Vitu**	= Things
Chura	= A frog	*Vyura*	= *Frogs*

There is generally an idea of smallness connected with this class, though **Kifaru** and **Kiboko** hardly bear this out, but

Mlima ..	A mountain	**Kilima**[1]	A hill
Mwiko ..	A large wooden spoon	**Kijiko** ..	A small spoon
Nyumba	A house	**Chumba**	A room
Sahani ..	A plate	**Kisahani**	A saucer

Correctly[2] *Adjectives agreeing with nouns of this class should also have the prefixes* **Ki-** *and* **Vi-** *for singular and plural.*

>   **Kitu kidogo kimoja** = One small thing
>   **Vitu vidogo viwili** = Two small things

Other variables should take the following forms with this class of noun.

Singular ·		Plural		Singular		Plural	
This	*Hiki*	*These*	*Hivi*	*That*	*Kile*	*Those*	*Vile*
My	*Changu*		*Vyangu*	*Thy*	*Chako*		*Vyako*
His or				*Our*	*Chetu*		*Vyetu*
her	*Chake*		*Vyake*	*Their*	*Chao*		*Vyao*
Your	*Chenu*		*Vyenu*	*All*	*Chote*		*Vyote*
Of	*Cha*		*Vya*				

TRANSLATE (using correct forms).—Three tall hills. All these spoons are yours. This thing is not mine, and those five are the cook's. Put away all those things in his room. I want a large saucer. To eat raw meat is a bad thing.

---

[1] Though the highest mountain in Africa is called **Kilima Njaro** !

[2] " Adjectives " include the six variable numerals, 1, 2, 3, 4, 5, and 8, which become **Kimoja, Viwili, Vitatu, Vine, Vitano** and **Vinane.** But **Sita, Saba,** etc., never vary.

In general practice, **Kidogo-Vidogo** = Small, is the only adjective that is correctly used with this class, the other adjectives being as already learnt.

Adjectives used adverbially, or when without a noun, are generally put unto this class. Also adjectives denoting nationality.

You cook very badly !	**Wapika kibaya sana !**
Good ! Excellent !	**Vyema ! Vizuri !**
European	**Kizungu** or **Ya kizungu**
Swahili	**Kiswahili**
Barbarous	**Kishenzi** or **Ya kishenzi**
English	**Kiingereza**
[1] **Hivi** is used to mean	Like this or thus
Vile-vile ,, ,,	Like that, or the same
Sasa hivi ,, ,,	Immediately
Bado kidogo ,, ,,	Not quite yet

TRANSLATE.—This man is a Swahili, he knows all the words (**maneno**) of Swahili. This European prefers European medicines, but we blacks prefer native (barbarous) medicines. You have sewn up my clothes very nicely. It does not do to be late like this, and you, cook, you were late as well. Go to your work immediately. Good ! You are doing your work well nowadays.

SUBSTANTIVES OF THE **Ki-, Vi-** CLASS.

Learn this vocabulary.

Kikapu ..	Basket	**Kilima** ..	Hill
Kitanda	Bedstead	**Kiboko**	Hippopotamus
Kitabu ..	Book	**Kibanda**	Hut
Viatu ..	Boots	**Chuma** ..	Iron
Kifungo	Button	**Kisu** ..	Knife
Kiti ..	Chair	**Choo** ..	Latrine
Kifua ..	Chest (breast)	**Kifuniko**	Lid. Cover
Kitambaa	Cloth	**Kioo** ..	Looking-glass
Kizibo ..	Cork	**Kibiriti**	box of Matches
Kikombe	Cup	**Kibaba** ..	Measure (of volume)
Kidole ..	Finger	**Kinanda**	Musical Instrument
Kiroboto	Flea	**Kioga** ..	Mushroom
Chakula	Food	**Vitunguu**	Onions
Chura ..	Frog	**Kipande**	Piece
Kipini ..	Handle	**Kiko** ..	tobacco Pipe
Kichwa	Head	**Kifuko** ..	Pocket

[1] **Hivi-hivi** is often used to mean "in disorder," "topsy-turvy," "all anyhow."

Viazi ..	Potatoes	Kichungo	Sieve
Kitambaa	Rag	Kidonda	Sore
Chumba	Room	Kijiko ..	Spoon
Kifaru ..	Rhinoceros	Kitu ..	Thing
Kisahani	Saucer	Kidole ..	Toe
Kibanda	Shed	Chuma ..	Tool
Viatu ..	Shoes	Kijana ..	Youngster

Kiboko, also means a short thick whip made of Hippopotamus, or other, hide.

Kipande also means the Registration Certificate, similar to a European's passport, that is issued to any adult male native who leaves his native Reserve.

Kitambaa—this word has a very broad meaning which includes almost any cloth substance other than clothes and blankets.

TRANSLATE, using the general form of adjectives, etc.—These are my baskets. Take those shoes off the bed. I do not like this book even a little. Clean my boots at once ! I have a cold (I a sick-man of the chest). You must fasten every button. This chair is not broken. Why is the cork lost ? Bring three cups. Your finger is swollen. Bring food immediately. The door handle has come off. My head is hurting me very much. This hill is very high. A hippopotamas has destroyed our hut. Undo this lid with a knife, then bring the matches. The iron fell and broke this looking-glass into many pieces. I do not like onions, but I like potatoes and mushrooms. Give me another hand towel and take these curtains to the mistress, in the dining room. Boy ! I have lost my pipe. I see it, master, on the piano. If you listen hard you will be able to hear the rhinoceros making a noise. Clean these shoes again with black polish (colour). This youth's sore is healing nicely. Bring me seven spoons and two saucers. These are the tools of my motor-car. The latrine is full of fleas. That man is a witch-doctor, see the frog in his pocket. This sieve is useless, you must sift it again. Look after this youngster, he does not yet know his work.

LOCATIVE CASE.

Whenever, in a sentence, the idea of position is intended in connection with a noun, that noun may be put into the locative case by adding a final **-ni** to it. The accentuated syllable of the word is thereby altered in conformity with the normal rule

Nyumba = A house. **Nyumbani** = In the house, or To, from, at, by (etc.) the house.

The locative case is not used when a noun has an adjective following it, or when it represents an animal or person.

The following nouns are those most generally used with the locative case.

Mlango	Door	**Mlangoni**	At, by, from, in, to, etc., the Doorway
Shamba	Farm Field	**Shambani**	,, ,, ,, ,, ,, on ,, ,, Farm
Nyumba	House	**Nyumbani**	,, ,, ,, ,, ,, ,, ,, ,, House
Soko	Market	**Sokoni**	, ,,, ,, ,, ,, ,, ,, ,, Market
Mlima	Mountain	**Mlimani**	,, ,, ,, ,, ,, ,, ,, ., Mountain
Njia	Road	**Njiani**	,, ,, ,, ,, ,, ,, ,, . Road
Duka	Shop	**Dukani**	,, ,, ,, ,, ,, ,, ,, ,, Shop
Meza	Table	**Mezani**	,, ,, ,, ,, ,, ,, ,, ,, Table

There are also the following with rather special meanings:

Porini or **Upolini**[1]		Out in the bush
Kilindini ..	..	At the deep water
Musitoni ..	..	In the forest
Mkononi ..	..	In the hand
Jikoni ..	..	The kitchen[2]
Mtoni ..	..	The river
Kivulini ..	..	In the shade
Seduleni ..	..	In the sitting-room, or just, The sitting-room
Juani ..	..	In the sunlight
Cheroni[3] ..	..	Dung. Manure
Chini[4] ..	..	On the ground. Down

The possessive pronouns, when used with a noun in the locative case, take a prefix of **Mw-** *when position within is intended,* and **Kw-** in other cases.

> *In my house* = *Nyumbani mwangu*
> To (etc.) my house = **Nyumbani kwangu**

The **Mw-** *prefix is seldom heard up-country, but one example sometimes met is* **Humo** = In there, as against **Huko** = Over there.

Kwangu, Kwako, Kwake, Kwetu and **Kwao** are often used by themselves to mean " At my house," " At your house," etc., or even " To me," " To you," etc., where motion is intended.

---

[1] Africans, like the Chinese, often confuse " L " and " R."
[2] Literally **Jiko** = Fireplace, therefore **Jikoni** = At the fireplace.
[3] A corruption of **Chooni** = In the latrine.
[4] **Inchi** = Land Ground. Hence the abreviation from **Inchini.**

TRANSLATE.—Put down my boots at the door.   The master is
not at home, he has gone on to the farm.   We are going to our
house, you go to yours !   Perhaps I will try to buy bananas in
the market, if I can not get them there I will go to the shop.
He had come from the mountain, he had passed over the river,
and when I met him he was running along the road.   Put the
coffee on the table in the sitting-room.   He came to me with
his Registration certificate in his hand.   I saw two Rhinos
out in the bush, I hear that you have speared many in the forest
often.   Tell the cook I wish to inspect the kitchen.   Dry these
clothes in the sun, but put away these in the shade.

Ma- CLASS.

There is another class of nouns which make their plural by
a prefix of **Ma-**.

$$\textbf{Yai} = \text{An egg} \qquad \textbf{Mayai} = \text{Eggs}$$

*Correctly adjectives with this class should have no prefix with the
singular and a prefix of* **Ma-** *with the plural.*

Maji mazuri = Good water

The pronoun prefixes are **Li-** *for singular, and* **Ya-** *for plural
so the demonstratives become :—*

Singular		Plural	
This	*Hili*	*These*	*Haya*
That	*Lile*	*Those*	*Yale*
Of	*La*		**Ya**
All	*Lote*		**Yote**
My	*Langu*		**Yangu**
Thy	*Lako*		**Yako**
		etc.	

It will strike = *Litapiga*   *They will strike* = *Yatapiga*

In general practice the form of demonstrative, etc., are as
those for the normal **N-** class.

But **Gari la mosh** = Waggon of smoke, *i.e.*, railway train.

Certain of the nouns are only used in their plural forms, and
some are more generally used either in the singular or plural

to express both cases. The uncommon forms are shown in italics in the following vocabulary.

Shauri, *Mashauri*	Affair	**Shimo**	..	Hole
Mapatano	Agreement	**Majani**	..	Leaves
Lozi, **Malozi** ..	Almonds	**Soko** ..	..	Market
Jibu, **Majibu** ..	Answer	**Maziwa**	..	Milk
Majivu	Burnt out ashes	**Jina,** *Majina* ..		Name
Makusanyiko ..	Assembly	**Shingo**	..	Neck
Shoka, *Mashoka*	Axe	**Mafuta**	..	Oil
Maganda ..	Bark. Rind			
Pipa, *Mapipa* ..	Barrel	**Chungwa**		
Chupa, *Machupa*	Bottle	**Machungwa**		Orange
Bakuli	Small bowl	**Papayi**	..	Pawpaw
Sanduku ..	Box	**Nanasi**		
Gari	Cart	**Mananasi**		Pineapple
Makaa	Charcoal	**Shimo**	..	Pit
	Embers	**Shamba**	..	Plantation
Kanisa	Church	**Jembe**		
Sikio, **Masikio** ..	Ears	*Majembe*	..	Plough
		Sufuria	..	metal cooking
Yai, **Mayai** ..	Eggs			Pot
Jicho[1], **Macho** ..	Eyes	**Tumbo**	..	Stomach. Inside
Shamba	Farm. Culti-	*Jiwe*[1], **Mawe** ..		Stones
	vated area	**Jua**		Sun
Mafuta	Fat	*Jino*[3], **Meno** ..		Teeth
Kosa, Makosa ..	Fault	**Gari**		Waggon
Ua, **Maua** ..	Flowers	**Maji**		Water
Matunda ..	Fruit	**Bibi**[4] ..		Native wife
Majani	Grass	**Dirisha** ..		Window
Jembe[2], *Majembe*	Hoe	*Neno,* **Maneno**		Words

TRANSLATE.—The train has already arrived. Now I will write out your agreement. The almond trees are in fruit. Where is the answer to my letter ? Ashes are white, but cinders are black. Take this axe and take the bark off that tree and put it in those barrels. You have forgotten to bring the slop basin. This (man) has a stomach ache. Throw away the bottle. Do you see that waggon with sixteen oxen ? Bring some (red-hot) ashes to start the fire. Master, we want to build a church on the farm.

---

[1] Single syllable words of this class take a prefix of **Ji-** which they drop again in the plural form.

[2] Is also used as a verb = To hoe.

[3] **Meno** is a contraction, for euphony, of **Maino.**

[4] *Bibi is really a term of respect meaning lady, mistress, madam, etc., but it has now degenerated into meaning a native woman in distinction to Memsaab, a European woman.*

You have broken all the eggs again, where are your ears and eyes ? Stop talking (leave words), it is just your fault. Pick up all the flowers and fruit and send them to my place. The plough is out of action. Just hoe up this grass. You, go to the market to buy the milk and lamp oil, because I am going to a meeting of the Europeans. Who are you ? I'm just a man ! Yes, but what is your name ? (your name is who ?) Where is the tin of fat and the box of soap ? I see them both on the table. I am ill as to the neck. I am looking for some plough oil. I like oranges very much, give me one orange, also a pawpaw and two pineapples. Fill in all the holes on the plantation. The cooking pot is full of water. The sun is very strong, the stones are exceedingly hot. This man's wife brings an affair (to be adjudicated) master, a small affair only, not (one of) many words. Her teeth are beautiful. The waggon pole is broken. Open the window.

The word **Na** = And or With, sometimes coalesces with a contracted form of the personal pronouns to make one word.

With me .. .. **Nami**	*With us* .. .. *Nasi*
With you .. .. **Nawe**	*With you* .. .. *Nanyi*
With him or her .. **Naye**	*With them* .. .. *Nao*
With it (" N " class) .. **Nayo**	*With them* (" N " class) *Nazo*

THE VERBS " TO BE " AND " TO HAVE."

The present tense of the verb " to Be " is generally expressed either by simple omission, as in previous exercises, or by the word **Iko** when a stronger sense is required, or when position is intended. There is also a weak form **Ni** when the verb is only a connecting link between two nouns, or between a noun and an adjective or adverb.

It is here	**Iko hapa**	It is not here *Hapana*	} Hapana iko
Is there any water ?	**Iko maji ?**	There is none *Hakuna*	
The beautiful house	**Nyumba mzuri**	The house is beautiful	**Nyumba ni mzuri**
It is only me	**Ni mimi tu**		

For other tenses of the verb ' "To Be " the verb **Kuwa** is used.

I shall be	**Nitakuwa**	I shall not be	**Sitakuwa**
He was ..	**Alikuwa**		

There is no Swahili word for " Have " but " To be with "
takes its place.

He is with me	**Yeye iko nami**	
I have it	**Mimi iko nayo**	Or **Ninayo** if the " Have " is not to be emphasised
You have a hat	**Wewe iko na kofia** Or **Unayo kofia**	
I have not (got) it	**Mimi hapana iko nayo** Or **Sinayo**	
He will have a hoe	**Atakuwa na jembe**	

VOCABULARY.

Juzi ..	The day before yes-terday	**Juzi juzi** ..	The other day. Not long ago
Jana..	Yesterday	**Leo** ..	To-day
Kesho	Tomorrow	**Kesho kutwa**	The day after tomorrow

TRANSLATE.—Are there any bananas on the farm to-day ? Yes
sir, there are some, but the cook has taken all that are ripe (of
to ripen) and there remain only bad ones. Bad in what way ?
Some unripe, others have already gone rotten, those that are
good the cook has them in his house. Go to his (house) and
return with him, I want words with the cook, then perhaps I
shall have bananas at my (house) tomorrow. Bananas are good
fruit, the cook is a thief. The other day some hoes were missing
(at fault), I shall be here the day after tomorrow, you must have
all the tools here, because I want to count them once more,
and I am too busy (have many affairs) tomorrow. You have
got the knife, boy ? No sir, you have. No! I have not got it !

ADVERBS.

Learn this Vocabulary.

Juu ..	.. Above	**Taratibu** ..	Carefully
Kabisa	.. Absolutely	**Sawa-sawa** ..	Correctly
Baada	.. After (time)	**Mbali** ..	Distant
Tena ..	.. Again	**Chini** ..	Down
Sikuzote ..	Always	**Mbali** ..	Far off
Kando-kando	Around	**Upesi** ..	Fast
Nyuma[1] ..	Behind	**Zamani** ..	Formerly
Chini ..	Below	**Mbele**[1] ..	In front

[1] **Mbele** and **Nyuma** may be used rather differently from in English,
thus sometimes causing confusion. To give an illustration : If an
observer is looking at a tree, and a native is standing between him and
the tree, a European would say that the native was standing " in front
of " the tree (as if the tree were facing the observer), whereas a Swahili
would say that the native was standing " behind " the tree (as if the
tree were facing the same way as the observer) and *vice versa*.

Bure ..	.. Gratis	Sasa	Now
Sasa hivi	.. Immediately	Mara nyingi	Often
Ndani	... Inside	Inje	Outside
Halafu	.. Later	Kando-kando	at the Side
Zamani	.. Long ago	Tangu ..	Since
Tu ..	.. Merely	Pole-pole ..	Slowly
Kati-kati	.. In the middle, among	Bure	Surplus
		Pamoja ..	Together
Zaidi	.. More, greater quantity	Kweli ..	Truly
		Juu	Up
Ingine	.. More, another lot	Bure	Useless
Karibu	.. Near	Wakate ..	While

PREPOSITIONS.

Besides the four true prepositions, **Na, Ya, Kwa** and **Katika** there are others made from adverbs or nouns by the addition of **Ya.**

From adverbs **Juu ya** =Upon **Baada ya** =After (time), etc.
From nouns **Sababu** =Cause **Kwa sababu ya**=Because of
Mahali =Place **Mahali ya**[1] = In place of, instead of

Prepositions when used with a personal pronoun generally turn it into the passive pronoun, thus :—

Above me   becomes   **Juu yangu** (not **juu ya mimi**).
Behind you   „   **Nyuma yako**

TRANSLATE.—You know that the sun is above us. I will see him after lunch (food) behind the kitchen. Look here cook, since I ate that bread you made I have been very ill, because you cook extremely badly, also you are always late, if you do it again I shall sack (drive away) you altogether. Do you see that house down there among the trees ? I want you to go there immediately and as quickly as possible. I know that it is a long way, but formerly I often reached it in one hour. I was in front, but are brother was behind. A man does not get boots free if they my good ones. Your work is just wasted. Is your master inside ? Four bottles of milk are not enough, tomorrow I shall want more. Your father is outside, near the big tree, go and see and then return inside together with him. You say truly, there is a house in the middle and trees around it.

---

[1] *Should correctly be " Mahali pa " as mahali forms a class of its own with a prepositional prefix of " Pa." Hence " Hapa " = " Here," is really merely the demonstrative, " Mahali hapa " = " this place." " Mahali pale " = " that place," whence "Pale " comes to mean " There. " " Pale " is however seldom heard up-country.*

Adjectives derived from nouns or verbs. (*Correctly the* **Ya** *should be modified to agree with the preceding noun.*)

Alone	**Peke** with possessive pronoun		
i.e., By myself ..	**Peke Yangu**		
By yourself ..	**Peke Yako**		
By him, her, or			
itself ..	**Peke Yake**		
By ourselves ..	**Peke Yetu**		
By yourselves ..	**Peke Yenu**		
By themselves ..	**Peke Yao**		
Ancient	**Ya Zamani**		
Blue	**Rangi ya Buluu.** *Rangi ya Samawi*		
Cold	**Ya Baridi**		
European (of Europeans)	**Ya Kizungu** or **Ya Wazungu**		
European (of Europe) ..	**Ya Ulaya**		
Green	**Rangi ya majani**		
Hot	**Ya Moto**	First (beginning)	**Ya Kwanza**
[1]Last	**Ya Mwisho**	First (number one)	**Ya Mosi**
Left-hand ..	**Ya Kushoto**	Second	**Ya Pili**
Rich	**Wa Mali**	Third	**Ya Tatu**
Right-hand ..	**Ya Kulia**	Fourth	**Ya Ine**
Strong	**Na Nguvu**	Fifth	**Ta Tano**
True	**Ya Kweli**	Sixth	**Ya Sita**
Uncivilized ..	**Ya Kishenzi**	etc.	etc.
Wet	**Maji-maji**		

European customs. **Dasturi ya Wazungu,** *i.e.,* of the Europeans.
European chair. **Kiti ya Kizungu,** *i.e.,* of the European pattern.
European tree. **Miti ya Ulaya[2],** *i.e.,* of Europe.

Other adjectives that have no variable prefixes are :—

Alike	**Sawa-sawa**	Level	**Sawa-sawa**
Cheap	**Rahisi**	Plenty	**Tele**
Clean	**Safi**	Poor	**Maskini**
Equal	**Sawa-sawa**	Ready	**Tayari**
Expensive ..	**Gali**	Straight	**Sawa-sawa**
		Smartly dressed	**Maridadi**

TRANSLATE.—I shall stay here by myself, but you yourself, when ready, will go, together with the cook, to that European house on the hill. I know truly that it is very ancient but you two will clean it and arrange it correctly, because my friend will sleep there. He is a very rich man and he likes everything clean and straight, he does not like things uncivilised like a poor (man). Give him plenty of hot water and see that you are dressed smartly.

---

[1] Last Year is often translated as **Mwaka wa jana.**
[2] **Miti ya Ulaya** has come to mean rather especially gum trees or wattle trees though it may be used of almost any tree foreign to Africa.

Put away the cheap window curtains of calico and take with you those expensive ones, put the green ones on the left-hand window and the blue ones on the right-hand window, then when all is ready give me news, and I will come and inspect it. The herdsman is cold and his cattle are wet, but it does not matter he is truly a strong man. The first ox is black, the last one is white, the second and the sixth are red. I did it last month.

TIME.

As, on the Equator, the sun always rises and sets at about 6 a.m. and 6 p.m., this is taken as the beginning of the day and night, and the hours are counted from then, as in Biblical times.

Thus :—

7 o'clock	is	**Saa Moja**
8	„ „	**Saa Mbili**
9	„ „	**Saa Tatu, etc.**
12	„ „	**Saa Sita, etc.**
3	„ „	**Saa Tisa, etc.**

6 o'clock itself is **Saa Kumi na Mbili**; though the Arabic form **Saa thenashara** is often used.

The unsophisticated African does not understand accurate measurement of time, he measures it by the height of the sun above the horizon, and **Saa Moja** means to him "the first hour" as in the Bible, and may be almost any time between 6 and 7 o'clock. Originally he had no conception of half or quarter hours, though Europeans are altering this, and those natives most in touch with Europeans are now necessarily beginning to conform to European ideas.

Mchana	..	Daylight	**Asubuhi**	..	Morning
Usiku ..	..	Night-time	**Jioni**	..	Evening

The hours of darkness may have the word **Usiku** added, to distinguish from the hours of daylight.

TRANSLATE.—What is the time ? Three o'clock. Seven o'clock. Half past four. 7.30 p.m. 5 a.m. Midnight. 5 p.m. 8 a.m. 11 a.m. 10.30 p.m. Six o'clock in the evening. Six o'clock in the morning.

The days of the week start on Saturday, and are numbered as far as Wednesday.

Saturday ..	**Juma mosi**
Sunday ..	**Juma pili**
Monday ..	**Juma tatu**
Tuesday ..	**Juma ine**
Wednesday	**Juma tano**
Thursday	**Alhamisi**
Friday ..	**Jumaa,** or **Siku ya Jumaa**

The true African " day " starts at sunset, as in all Mohammedan countries, so that to the un-Europeanised African " 7 p.m. on Friday evening," would be **Saa moja usiku, juma mosi.** " One hour of night, Saturday."

Jumaa means " week," but now the English word is more generally used among natives, all of whom are becoming ever more Europeanised.

TRANSLATE.—You two children will attend to the fruit trees for the whole of daylight, you (singular) will come very (early in the) morning when the sun has not yet appeared, this one will come at midday until night, you must not leave until this one arrives. Your work is to drive away the birds and see that they do not eat the fruit. You two will do it on Monday, Wednesday, Friday and Sunday of this week, and two other children will do it on Tuesday, Thursday and Saturday. Yesterday was Monday, the day after tomorrow will be Thursday. This year Christmas is on Friday.

MONEY.

East African money has had many vicissitudes, all of which have left their mark on Swahili monetary terms.

The original currency was based on the Austrian " Maria Theresa " Thaler, or dollar of 1780 A.D., which, until the Italian invasion, was still minted for use in Abyssinia.

The British regime introduced and legalised the Indian rupee **Rupia** with silver pieces for half-rupee **Nusu** and quarter-rupee **Sumuni.** (The latter name comes from the word **Thumuni** = an eighth part (Arabic), as it was taken as one eighth part of a Maria Theresa dollar, the dollar being actually worth slightly more than two rupees.) There were also small bronze coins called Pice **Pesa.** Later annas and pies were abolished and the rupee was divided into 100 cents **Senti**, the **Nusu** and **Sumuni** becoming the 50-cent and 25-cent pieces respectively, there were also ten-cent, five-cent and one-cent pieces made of nickel with a central hole for threading on string.

After the first war, when currencies were fluctuating violently and the rupee was rising in value inordinately, East Africa pegged its currency to sterling by changing its rupee into a florin, but next year the florin was abolished and a shilling of the same size, but of poorer silver, was introduced. The shilling also was divided into 100 cents, with silver 50-cent pieces, and ten-cent, five-cent and one-cent pieces, similar to the previous ones, but of bronze instead of nickel.

The older natives have not managed to keep pace with these changes, and they still think in rupees and cents of a rupee, they thus consider the shilling to be a **Nusu** or half-rupee, the 50-cent piece is universally named **Sumuni**, and 25 cents is often called **Pesa Nane**. Confusion is thus caused by the older natives calling and thinking of a ten-cent piece as **Senti Tano** instead of **Senti Kumi**.

To summarise the monetary vocabulary we get :—

English	Modern form	Old-fashioned form
One cent	**Senti moja**	**Nusu Senti**
Ten cents ..	**Senti kumi**	**Senti tano**
Twenty-five cents	**Senti ishirini na tano**, or **Pesa nane**	**Pesa nane**
Fifty cents ..	**Sumuni**	**Sumuni**
Shilling	**Shilingi**	**Nusu rupia**
Two shillings ..	**Shilingi mbili**	**Rupia moja**
Money	**Shilingi** or **Rupia**	**Rupia**
One and sixpence	**Shilingi moja na nusu** ..	**Nus na sumuni**

Measures of weight are :—

Ratili[1]	Pound
Frasla	Thirty-six pounds
Mzigo	Load of sixty pounds
Gunia (maize) ..	Bag of 200lbs. net. (203lbs. gross)
Kibaba ya Posho	The day's ration of maize meal

The **Kibaba**, or measure for **Posho**, used to be a 1 lb. Lipton's tea tin which held just about 2 lbs. of **Posho**, (maize meal). These are now no longer available and farmers generally cut down

---

[1] **Ratili** is also generally used to mean the weighing machine as well, though the correct word is **Mizani**.

taller tins until they hold the standard 2 lbs. of **Posho** when heaped up.

The **Frasla** is only used for native produce, and not for maize.

VOCABULARY.

Ku-vuna ..	To harvest, pick	**Karani** ..	Clerk, manager
Mshahara ..	Wages, pay	**Neopara** ..	Head-man
Bakshishi ..	Reward, tip	**Ndito** ..	Unmarried girl
Dudu ..	Insect		

Translate.—I will give out pay now, but first I will give the women their rewards for the tins of coffee they have picked, ten cents for each tin. Tell the clerk to see that each tin is of ripe coffee only. If a woman brings a tin with much unripe coffee I shall refuse her reward. Now, you old man, your pay is ten shillings, but you have already borrowed three, there remain seven shillings. How much, master ? Three and a half rupees. Tell the head-man to give out Posho, women of three tins get a whole measure, but those of two tins get half a measure, and those of only one tin do not get any. This girl has two tins, twenty cents, and this woman, her mother, has three tins, thirty cents, I will give them fifty cents together, as the cents are nearly finished. Shs 6/30 cts., 8/20, 4/35, 11/50, 5/25, 15/75. Seventy-five cents are fifty cents and twenty-five cents. There are plenty of insects here.

SUBSTANTIVES OF THE U CLASS.

Correctly, this class have a singular in **U-**, *or* **W-** *before a vowel, and a plural commencing with* **N-**, *or* **Ny-** *before a vowel. In the singular, adjectives, etc., with this class are as with the singular of the* **M-** *Inanimate class, and in the plural they are as with the plural of the* **N-** *class.*

i.e., Singular	*Wa*	*Of*	*Huu*	*This*	*Mzuri*	*Beautiful*
Plural	*Za*	*Of*	*Hizi*	*These*	*Nzuri*	*Beautiful*

But generally the usual forms as with the **N-** class singular are used.

The nouns of this class include Abstract Ideas and Qualities.

Although the plurals of this class should normally commence with **N-** *yet those plurals in actual use almost all have roots beginning with those consonants which, in Swahili, will not tolerate an* **N-** *before them, so the prefix becomes suppressed.*

VOCABULARY.

Showing plural form when in use.

	Singular	Plural			Singular	Plural
Broom ..	Ufagio ..	Fagio		Night ..	Usiku ..	
Face ..	Uso			Nonsense	Upuuzi	
Falsehood	Urongo			Plank ..	Ubau ..	Mbau
Firewood		Kuni		Porridge ..	Ugali ..	
Flour ..	Unga ..			Razor ..	Wembe	
Fork ..	Uma ..			Side ..	Upande	
Gruel ..	Uji ..			String ..	Uzi ..	
Illness ..	Ugonjwa			Sword ..	Upanga	Panga
Ink ..	Wino ..			Tongue ..	Ulimi	
Key ..	Ufunguo	Funguo		Wall ..	Ukuta..	
Lamp Wick	Utambi	Tambi		Wind ..	Upepo	
Length ..	Urefu ..			Witchcraft	Uchawi	

COMPARISON OF ADJECTIVES.

This can be expressed by **Sana** for a simple comparative, or by **Kuliko** in the cases in which we would use " Than." For the Superlative **Kabisa** may be used. The verb **Kushinda** is also used to mean that one thing is better in its way than another.

TRANSLATE.—The first bundle is heavy, the second is heavier, but the third is the heaviest. This razor is sharper than that one ; what do you say ? I say, this razor beats that one. Bring a broom and sweep the sitting-room, there is firewood on the floor. This is the face-towel. That is just his lie, master, he stole the flour to prepare his gruel or porridge. What is your illness ? Do you sleep at night ? Show me your tongue. don't know, what do you think it is ? Witchcraft ? No, that's just nonsense. Plane these planks then cut them to this length, measure them equal to this board, that done use them to build a wall over there. Where are the keys of this box ? I want to look for a lamp-wick. When you lay the table, put the knives on the right side of the plate, and the forks on the left side. The ink has dried up. Your sword is as sharp as a razor. The wind has carried away the string, bring me a longer one.

ENGLISH WORDS.

Many English words have become incorporated in up-country Swahili, though some have become greatly distorted in the process.

As Bantu words always end in a vowel, English words, when adopted, are given a fina lvowel when necessary.

Thus : Jam becomes **Jami.**   Sheet becomes **Shiti or Siti.**

The accent is sometimes kept as in English, thus breaking the normal rule of accentuating the one from last vowel.

Cupboard   .. **Kábadi**   Socks   .. **Sókisi**

The amount by which English words are distorted depends on the native concerned, the form given below is intended to be the greatest distortion normally met, anything between it, and the true English may be used.

Natives have a tendency to confuse **r** and **l, k** and **g,** and **sh** and **s;** and when in the English several consonants come together they are apt to separate them by inserting an extra vowel.

The following list is more an illustration of the way in which natives alter English words, than a comprehensive vocabulary of them.

The accentuated syllable is shown in those cases in which it deviates from the normal.

Bath..	..	**Bafu**	Gaol ..	**Jeli**
Biscuit	..	**Bísikoti**	Inspection	**Peksen**
Blanket	..	**Baringeti**	Lemonade	**Nimeleti**
Washing blue		**Buluu**	Post-office	**Pósita**
Brake	..	**Feregi**	P.W.D. ..	**Peloti**
Brush	..	**Barasi**	Report ..	**Loboti**
Cheese	..	**Chizi or Kizi**	School ..	**Sikulu**
Cupboard	..	**Kábadi**	Socks ..	**Sókisi**
Doctor	..	**Dakitari or Nekitari**	Starch ..	**Sitaki**
Driver	..	**Ndaraiba or Dereva**	Store ..	**Sitoa**
Fall-in	..	**Foleni**	Tin-opener	**Tínikata**
Frying-pan	..	**Faraipani**	Week ..	**Wiki**

There are also the following, in which a modified form of one English word is used to express another.

Camera	.. ..	**Piksha**	Photograph ..	**Piksha**
Cigarette	.. ..	**Sigara**	Daily task, piece work	**Futi**[2]
Knitted vest, jumper		**Fulana**[1]	Safety-pin	**Pini**
Lettuce	.. ..	**Saladi**	Steam-ship	**Meli**[4]
Measuring tape, rule		**Futi**[2]	Native servant ..	**Boy**
Peas ..	.. ..	**Binzi**[3]	Savoury	**Tosti**[5]

TRANSLATE[6].—Boy, get my bath ready, and don't put in as much hot water as you did yesterday, I like it hot, but not too hot. To wash the clothes you will want soap, blue and starch, come to the store and I will give you them, see that my sheets and blankets are dry. Tell the driver not to tighten the wagon's brakes so much, I want the wheels to be able to turn. You have not yet finished your piece work I measured, you must hoe this line of peas and those lettuces. This cupboard smells of cheese, bring brushes and water and scrub its shelves. I want you to go to the Post-Office with these letters, and as you pass the school on the way give the teacher this coat and these socks and jumper. Take this letter to the doctor to say that I want some quinine for the men for another week, perhaps you will find him at the gaol. The visitor (European) wants some biscuits and lemonade. Sir, give me a safety-pin to take the insects out of my foot. Bring me my book of photographs and that yard measure. Tell the cook to bring a frying-pan and a tin-opener. He reports that the P.W.D. will inspect his hut.

There now only remains a rather long vocabulary of words to learn, and the student who has conscientiously worked through to the end will speak better Swahili than the average settler of many years standing. Military students have a further stage to go.

---

[1] From " Flannel."

[2] From " Foot " measurement.

[3] From " Beans," beans are **Maharagwe** and peas are **Binzi**.

[4] From " Mail-boat."

[5] " First Toastie " = Appetisers before Dinner.
" Second Toastie " = Savoury at end of Dinner.

[6] Europeans naturally adhere more closely to the correct English forms of these words than do natives, therefore in the key to this exercise some less extreme forms have been used for words that vary.

Learn this vocabulary, sixteen words at a time.

Alcoholic liquor	Tembo	Dog	'Mbwa
Artisan ..	Fundi	Donkey ..	Punda
Baboon ..	Nyani	Drain	Fereji
Ball	Mpira	Duck	Bata
Barren cow ..	Ngombe Malaya	Dung	Mavi
		Dust	Vumbi
Beads	Ushanga	Dutchman, Boer	Bwana Kaburu
Beans	Maharagwe	Earth⁴	Udongo
Belt	Mishipi	Early	Mapema
Breath	Pumuzi	Easy	Rahisi
Bricks	Matofali	Elephant ..	Tembo
Bridge	Daraja	England ..	Ungereza
Brother-in-law¹	Shemeji	Englishmen ..	Wangereza
Buck	Swara	English (things)	Kiingereza
Buffalo ..	Mbogo	Enough ..	Basi
Bush-buck ..	Bongo	Envelope ..	Bahasa
Playing cards ..	Karata		

Cat	Paka	False accusation	Fitina
Catch hold², To	Ku-shika	Ring-fence ..	Boma
Chain	Nyororo	Fever	Homa
Chicken ..	Kuku	Firm. Steady ..	Imara
Chisel	Patasi	Flea	Kiroboto
Circumcised, To		Fowl	Kuku
become ..	Ku-tahiri	Giraffe ..	Twiga
Cock	Jogoo	Glass. Tumbler	Bilauri
Dried Coffee		Gourd	Kibuyu
Cherries ..	Buni	Government ..	Serikali
Corrugated iron	Mabati	Groom ..	Sais
Crooked ..	Goi-goi	Guinea-fowl ..	Kanga
Crowbar ..	Mitalimbo	Hair	Nywele
Cut to a point,		Hare	Sangura
To	Ku-chonga	Harlot	Malaya
Curry powder	Binzari	Hartebeest ..	Kongoni
Diarrhoea, To			
have ..	Ku-hara		
Dirt. Dirty ..	Chafu		
Discharge a ser-		Heifer	Mtamba
vant³, To ..	Ku-futa	Horse	Farasi

---

¹ Or sister-in-law.

² **Ku-kamata** is more used than **ku-shika**.

³ Used of signing off a labourer by completing the Discharge Column in his Registration Certificate.

⁴ **Udongo** generally means earth mixed with water, dry earth would normally be **Mchanga** = Sand.

Hyaena	Fisi. Nyangau	Professional, A	Fundi
Idiot	Pumbavu	Rat	Panya
In vain	Bure	Ribs	Mbavu
Indian, man	Muhindi	Rice	Mchele
Indian corn.		Roots	Mizizi
Maize	Mahindi		
Indiarubber[1]	Mpira	Sack	Gunia
Inoculate, To	Ku-chanja	Saddle	Matandiko
Intentionally	Makusudi	Salt	Chumvi
Iron sheeting	Mabati	Sand	Mchanga
Kettle	Birika	Saw	Msumeno
Kidney	Figo	Scissors	Makasi
Leave of absence	Ruksa	Seed	Mbegu
Lemon	Ndimu. Limau	Shave, To	Ku-nyoa
Leopard	Chui	Sieve, A	Kichungo
		Sleep (noun)	Singizi
Lion	Simba	Soldier	Askari
Liver	Ini	Long thin Stick	Fito
Good-luck	Bahati	Stir, To	Ku-koroga
Maize	Mahindi	Sugar	Sukari
Maize meal	Posho	Tarpaulin	Chandarua
Milk a cow, To	Ku-kama	Tax	Kodi
	ngombe	Tent-peg	Kigingi
Millet (Eleusine)	Wimbi		
Millet (Kaffir-			
corn)	Mtama	Thank-you	Asante
Mouse	Panya	Tobacco	Tumbaku
Move House, To	Ku-hama	Trample on, To	Ku-kanyaga
Much	Tele	Trestle-work	
Mud	Matope	Bench	Kitanda
Nail (wire)	Msumari	Tribe	Kabila
Nothing	Hapana Kitu	Trousers	Suruali
Pair	Jozi	Tyre	Mpira
Peg	Kigingi	Vomit, To	Ku-tapika
Pepper	Pili-pili	Washerman	Dobi
		Water-buck	Nkulu
Perspiration	Jasho	Wattle, or Gum	
Pickaxe	Sururu	Trees	Miti ya Ulaya
Pig	Nguruwe	Wedding	Arusi
Water Pipe	Fereji	Weighing	
Place	Mahali	Machine	Ratili
Plant, To	Ku-panda	Wheel	
Policeman	Askari	Gurudumu	Mguu
Porter	Mpagazi	Worthless fellow	Mugoi-goi
Porters	Wapagazi	Wire	Sengenge
Pregnancy	Mimba	Zebra	Punda-Milia
Price	Bei, Kiasi		

[1] Also anything usually made of rubber, i.e., ball, tyre, hot-water-bottle.

TRANSLATE.—The brick maker has manufactured much beer, he is playing cards with his brother-in-law the carpenter. Tell the Headman that I want to build a wagon shed, where is the tape-measure ? Bring pegs so as to mark out the place. Bring two crow-bars so as to dig holes for the posts. There are no crow-bars ? All right then, sharpen two thick sticks and use them instead of crow-bars. Send two men into the forest to cut two long pillars forked at the top, and two more to cut purlins (*fito*), two to look for strips of bark, and others to cut grass and others to cut posts. Then tomorrow give out two kerosine-tins and two hoes and put four men to trample earth, they can get the water from the water furrow. The baboons have eaten all the peas and beans, the fence round the garden must be increased. The clerk's daughter wants to buy some beads, she will sell a chicken, there is a wedding the day after tomorrow. You have not yet paid your tax, what tribe are you ? I will give out pay tomorrow evening. The elephants have trampled the furrow, and the water is running away. The Governor (Bwana Government) went on a journey last[1] month, and he shot one hippopotamus, two rhino, five harte beest, two water-buck, seven bush-buck, two topi, a leopard, an impala, two buffaloes and many buck ; he found a giraffe and two zebras killed by a lion, but their skins were spoilt by the hyaenas. On Tuesday he will go to shoot duck, guinea-fowl and perhaps hares. His porters have eaten meat until they were completely gorged. I hear that the barren cow has died, take off its skin, I will come to examine the heart, kidneys and liver. Tell the carpenter to bring a saw, a chisel, some wire, a hammer and nails, and you go yourself and fetch two picks. These two bags of maize-meal are full of weevil (insects). Put these four bags of seed maize on the trestles and cover with a tarpaulin. Give the groom this saddle and tell him to saddle the horse. The Indian asks for leave sir. Plant these gum trees near the cattle enclosure. I see you know how to milk a cow, you are quite a professional. The veterinary officer (cattle

---

[1] Last month = **Mwezi iliopita.** The "o" is the "Relative Pronoun." **Ilipita** = It passed. **Iliopita** = It which passed. The Relative is rarely used up-country, except in **Iliopita** and **Iliokwisha.** **Ujao** = "It which is to come," is sometimes used, *i.e.*, Next month = **Mwezi ujao** (or, **mwezi ingine**) and **Hio** or **Hivyo** are sometimes heard in place of **Hii** and **Hivi** when the meaning is "This with which we are concerned."

doctor) wants to inoculate all the heifers tomorrow.   Put some lemon juice (water) and sugar into a tumbler, stir it well and give it to the policeman.   Make some curry (Eng.) this evening, Have you got rice, salt, pepper and curry-powder ?   Sir, the washerman is bringing a false accusation against me, he says that I have stolen a shirt, a belt, some trousers and two pairs of socks. Take this pump and increase the air in the motor car tyres.   If you want leave to be circumcised I will sign off your registration certificate.   The cat had caught a mouse, but the dog drove her away and the mouse escaped.   Sir, I am ill of fever, at night I vomited and gave off much perspiration, sleep did not hold me.   Boy, my razor is spoilt, it will not cut even a little, I know you have used it to shave your head, and my scissors likewise, they are still dirty with your black hairs.   You have filled the kettle in vain, it is punctured and the tea has all run away. Plant this tree in this hole, cover the roots with earth and stamp it down, see that it is firm, then put on cattle manure.   The cock has many fleas, bring some lamp-oil and water to clean him, enough, only a little.   A mule is the child of a horse and a donkey. The wheels of the motor car are turning uselessly because there is much mud, put on chains.   When I give you tobacco as a reward you should say thank you.   The European pig has fallen into a pit, perhaps its ribs are broken.   This water-pipe, what is its price ?   Is it cheap ?   No, it comes from England, it is very expensive.   There are three Europeans outside, one Dutchman and two English.   A soldier came early and asked for some dried coffee cherry.   He is a perfect idiot, he knows nothing, he does everything crookedly.   The child who holds the head rope of the oxen is called the " **mshika-kamba.**"   Blow up this football. The road near the bridge is very bad, there is a lot of sand on it, take off the sand and dig a deep drain on each side.   Sir, I want to move my house, there is no good luck here, some time ago my wife started to have a baby, but at once she became very ill, her stomach purged greatly and then the baby came away, now she cannot have a child, she is but a harlot (barren woman), now I want to go to the farm of the tall bwana, but my sister-in-law will stay here and tend my millet and kaffir-corn. That is a worthless fowl-house, a leopard can easily break that, English fowls are expensive, I will build another of corrugated iron.   There is too much dust here throw some water over it, if there is no tin for the water you have a gourd.   All right, give me twenty-five cents, and I will give you a stamp, paper and envelope.

Certain machines are distinguished by the sounds that they make.

Tinka-tinka = A mill or other machine driven by an engine and belt.
Regi-regi   = A hand-mill or other machine turned by hand.
Sheki-sheki = A winower, or sieving machine with fore and aft motion.
Piki-piki   = A motor-bicycle.
Chuka-chuka = Sheki-sheki.

Ox harness parts are as follows :—

Yoki, the double yoke that passes over the necks of each pair of oxen.

Kesikei, the skeys, wooden side-pieces, which pass through holes in the yoke, each pair of which are fastened together by a strop which passes under the neck of the ox.

Sirupu, the strop, a twisted leather thong for joining the skeys under the neck of the yoked ox.

Terensi, the trance, a leather thong for fastening the trek-chain to the yoke.

Cedar Tree	.. **Mtaragwa**	Inform, to	.. **Ku-Harifu**
Cores, of maize		Olive Tree	.. **Matamayo**
cobs ..	.. **Visikoro**	Plague, the	.. **Tauni**
Fig Tree	.. **Makuyu**	Twist. to	.. **Ku-sokota**
Hard-wood Tree	**Msharagi**	Sim-sim oil	.. **Mafuta ya uto**

TRANSLATE.—To-morrow, early, I shall want eight boys to work the (hand) maize sheller.   They must stack the cores over there, and I want two girls to come to work to take off the remaining grains of maize by hand.   Sir, the shaker of the sheller is broken, the tin sieve is missing.   All right then, you must detail two extra boys to clean the maize in the other winnower.   Have you got enough petrol to start up the engine of the coffee pulper?   No, Sir ; the fundi asked for it the other day for his motor bicycle, and I gave him all of it.   The water-buck have been eating the maize and I have shot one, the skin will make good strops, and I will make some whips from the neck, is there any sim-sim oil for rubbing into the thongs ? Have we got plenty of head ropes and traces, or must we twist some more skins ? Boards of cedar split easily but they do not warp much, whereas Podo boards don't split so much but warp terribly.   There is an Olive pole here, cut out a yoke similar to that one, I will come back later to mark out the places to bore the holes for the skeys and the yoke iron.   I shall plant fig trees to cover the coffee bushes with their shade.

VOCABULARY. MILITARY TERMS.

Aeroplane	.. Ndege
Aim, to	.. Linga, ku-
Ammunition pouches	.. Mabete
Attack, to	.. Shambulia, ku-
Badge, a	.. Alama
Barbed wire	.. Sengenge ya miba
Barracks	.. Laini
Barren land	.. Jangwa
Battle, a	.. Mapigano
Bayonet	.. Singe
Beach ..	.. Pwani
Blank round	.. Baruti
Box, to	.. Piga ngumi, ku-
Brass ..	.. Shaba
Bugle ..	.. Buruji
Bugle call	.. Mlio wa buruji
Bugler ..	.. Burujee
Bullet ..	.. Risasi
open Bush country	.. Vishakani
Bush country ..	.. Porini
Cannon	.. Mzinga
Capture, to	.. Dumu, ku-
Cartridge (S.A.A.)	.. Risasi
Cartridge cases	Maganda
Cell ..	.. Korokoroni
Chin ..	.. Kidevu
Civilian	.. -a Raiya
Close in, to	.. Songa, ku-
Compass, magnetic	.. Dira
good Conduct	Adabu
good Conduct badge	.. Asanta
Cordite	.. Baruti
Corporal	.. Mbasha
Danger..	... Hatari
Dates ..	.. Tende
Defend, to	.. Linda, ku-
Desert country	Jangwa
Detail, to	.. Tuma, ku
Dry river bed	Mkondo
Dynamite	.. Baruti
Dysentery, to have ..	.. Hara damu, ku-
East ..	.. Mashariki
Elbow ..	.. Kisigino cha mkono
Electricity	.. Stima
Enemy..	.. Adui
Entry in conduct sheet	Kosa (Makosa)
Esprit de corps	Heshima
Even Numbers	Watu wa tu tu
Explode, to	.. Pasuka, ku-
Extinguish, to ..	.. Zima, ku
Field glasses	.. Darubini
Fist, a ..	.. Ngumi
Ford, a	.. Kivuko
Forest ..	.. Mwitu
Gonorrhea	.. Kisonono
Grenade	.. Bombu
Guard, to	.. Linda, ku-
Guardroom	.. Kwota gaad
Guide' ..	.. Kiongozi
Haversack	.. Mkoba
Heel..	.. Kisigino cha mguu
Homestead	.. Mtaa
Honour	.. Heshima
Horizon	.. Upeo wa macho
Island ..	.. Kisiwa
Judge, to	.. Hukumu, ku-
Knee, a	.. Goti
Knuckles	.. Konde
Lean upon, to	Tegemea, ku-
Machine gun, a	Bombom, Takataka
Marsh ..	.. Ziwa
Masai homestead	Manyata
Mufti ..	.. Nguo za raiya
North ..	.. Kaskazini

VOCABULARY. MILITARY TERMS—(*continued*).

Odd numbers..	Watu wa wan wan		Sergeant, a	.. Shawesh
Open bush			Shell, artillery, a	Risasi
country	.. Vishakani		Shell (bursting)	Baruti
Open country..	Mbugani		Shoulders	.. Mabega
Order, an	.. Amri		Shoulder strap,	Mshipi wa
Order, to	.. Amru, ku-		a	mabega
Orderly-room..	Maktab		Sink, to	.. Zama ku-
Pace, a..	.. Hatua		Sir ! ..	.. Fanti (Effendi)
Porter, a	.. Mpagazi		South ..	.. Kusini
Prisoner, a	.. Mabusu		Squeeze to	.. Kamua, ku-
Punishment	.. Athabu		Star, a..	.. Nyota
Ram home, to..	Shindilia, ku-		Straighten, to..	Nyosha, ku-
Rifle range, a ..	Shabaha		Stretcher, a	.. Machera
Recruit, a	.. Karutu		Stripe(N.C.O.'s)	Tepe
Regiment, the			Syphilis	.. Tego
(K.A.R.)	.. Keyaa			
Regulations	.. Kanuni		Telescope	.. Darubini
Reinforcements	Msaada		Town, a	.. Mji
Rice, cooked	.. Wali		Trench, a	.. Handaki
Rice, unpolished	Mpunga			
River bed, dry, a	Mkondo		Urinate, to	.. Kojoa, ku-
Rock, a	.. Mwamba			
Roll call	.. Tamaam		Valley, a	.. Bonde
Rust..	.. Kutu		Village, a	.. Kijiji
Scabbard, a	.. Ala		Visible, to	
Scout, to	.. Peleleza, ku-		become	.. Onekana, ku-
Sea, the	.. Bahari		Weapon, a	.. Silaha
Sentence			Well, a	.. Kisima
(judgment)	Hukumu		West ..	.. Mangaribi
Sentry, a	.. Mlinzi		Wound, a	.. Jeraha
			Yard, a, pace	.. Hatua

TRANSLATE.—To-morrow you will send the recruits to the rifle range. They will fire at a hundred yards, see that they aim properly, and that they squeeze the trigger slowly. How many cartridges have they in their ammunition pouches? If the enemy attack this town we will defend these trenches with machine-guns and grenades, we will erect barbed wire in front, and the artillery will also shell them. The bugler was late in sounding the bugle call. That soldier is drunk, confine him in the cell and bring him to Orderly-room as a prisoner to-morrow. He has a good conduct badge, but now that he has broken his good conduct he is spoiling the reputation of the Regiment and his punishment will be heavy. Put the shell in the breech then ram home with the rammer, and put in the cartridge. The layer will lay the gun through the telescope and fire it by electricity. Stand properly! Shoulders back, stick out your chest, raise your chin, straighten your knees! What is the matter with you? Yes Sir, I try to do my best, but I've lost heart (my spirit is dead). One Sergeant and two Corporals with ten soldiers will go to that Masai homestead. The path at first goes south, it crosses some barren land with two dry river beds, it passes some high rocks and turns to the east, it enters open country, and then open bush country, then bush country up to the river, and on the opposite bank of it there is forest. There is a ford to cross the river, and the track turns north along a valley at the end of which is the homestead of a Kikuyu. Leave his cultivated land on your left and you will arrive at the village, there is a well there. Beyond the town there is a marsh. If you stand on the beach and look at the sea you will see only water as far as the horizon, but if you go to the west in a steamer an island will soon become visible. A civilian tells me that there was a battle in the desert yesterday. There were many weapons on the ground, rifles, bayonets, scabbards, haver-sacks, and he picked up a compass and some field glasses. Bullets are of lead and the cartridge cases of brass. Lean your elbow on your knee. In the Barracks there are many men who have dysentery, others have syphilis or gonorrhœa and to urinate is painful. He has a wound in his heel, put him on a stretcher. He can not box, he has hurt his knuckles. Even numbers to the right, odd numbers to the left. Send this blank ammunition to the guard room. Shells were bursting on the bridge when the reinforcements captured the town. You did not obey my orders, you have five former entries in your conduct sheet, I sentence you to be reduced to the ranks. You will guard this cordite, according to regulations, until roll call. Tell the guide to tighten his shoulder straps. The porters have eaten all the rice and dates, never mind, we shall get some fresh rice to-morrow, but perhaps it will only be unpolished. He ordered me to report that all is correct. Their badge is a star.

Put out those lights! Two enemy submarines sank under the fire of our war-ships, but first they had sunk two of our steamers. Tell the sentry on the guns not to allow anyone to approach the ammunition with a cigarette because it is very dangerous. Detail an N.C.O. and six men to scout to the top of that hill. I am informed that there is plague in the town. Don't close up when you mark time!

SWAHILI-ENGLISH VOCABULARY.

A

Acha Ku-, to allow, let, let go, leave alone.
Adabu, good conduct.
Adui, enemy.
Afya, good health.
Akili, intelligence, skill.
Ala, a scabbard.
Alama, a mark, brand, badge
Alfajiri, very early in the morning, before dawn, cock-crow.
Alhamisi, Thursday.
Amani, peace.
ʾ Ambia Ku-, to tell.
* Amerikani, cotton sheeting.
Amka Ku- = Kuamuka, to awake.
Amri, an order.
Amsha Ku- = Kuamusha, to waken.
* Amuka Ku-, to awake (of one's own accord.
Amuru Ku-, to order.
Amusha Ku-, to waken (someone else).
* Andika Ku-, to write.
Angaika Ku-, to have to do without, to be troubled over.
* Angalia Ku-, to look at carefully, examine, beware, take notice, be careful.
* Anguka Ku-, to fall down.
Anika Ku-, to spread out to dry.
Anza Ku-, to begin.
Arifu Ku-, to inform.
* Arobaini, forty.
Arusi, a wedding.
* Asali, syrup, treacle, honey (sometimes wrongly used for the " bees ").
Asanta (Mil.) good conduct badge
* Asanti, thank you ! thanks !
* Askari, soldier, policeman.
* Asubuhi, early in the morning, the morning.

* Au, or Au . . Au, either . . or.
Aya, a native nurse, nursemaid.
Memsaab Aya, a European nurse.

B

* Baada, afterwards.
* Baba, a father.
Baba Mdogo, stepfather, uncle.
Babu, Indian or Goan clerk or official.
Badili Ku-, to change, alter.
Badilisa Ku-, to cause to be changed.
* Bado, not yet.
* Bado Kidogo, not quite yet, soon.
Bafu, a bath.
Bahari, the sea, a very large lake.
Bahasha, an envelope, satchel.
Bahati, good luck.
* Baki Ku, to remain, to be left over.
Bakuli, a small basin, a bowl.
Bali = Mbali, far, distant.
* Banda, a large shed, thatched house.
Bangi, bhang, Indian hemp.
* Bara-Bara, a broad open road.
Barafu, ice, hail, snow.
Barasi, (Eng.) brush.
Baraza, an official assembly of natives, verandah.
* Baridi, cold, draught, wind.
Baringeti, (Eng.) blanket.
* Barua, a letter, recommendation.
Baruti, dynamite, gun-powder, explosive, blank ammunition, a shell burst.
* Basi = Bas, enough ! that'll do ! all right !
Bata, pl. Mabata, a duck, goose.
Bata Mzinga, a turkey.
* Bau = Mbau, board, shelf, planking, a Native game

-Baya, bad.
Beba Ku-, to carry.
Bei, price.
Bendera, a flag.
Biashara, trade, merchandise.
* Bibi, native married woman, wife.
-Bichi, raw, unripe, green, under-
done.
Bidii, effort, enthusiasm.
Bila, without, except by.
Bilauri, tumbler, glass.
Binzi, peas.
Binzari, curry powder.
Birika, kettle, cistern, tank.
Bisikoti, (Eng.) biscuits.
-Bivu, ripe, well cooked.
* Boma, a ring-fence, an admini-
strative centre.
Bombom, a machine-gun
Bonde, a valley
-Bovu, over-ripe, rotten, bad.
Boy, (Eng.) native servant, native.
Buluu, (Eng.) washing blue, blue,
resident labourer's agreement
* Bunduki, a gun, rifle.
Buni, dried coffee cherry.
* Bure, free, gratis, surplus, useless,
in vain.
Buruji, a bugle, bugler.
Bustani, a flower garden.
* Bwana, master, husband, lord, sir,
a European man.
Bwana Mkubwa, the great lord,
the head European, the boss.
Bwana Mdogo, the master's
son, the lesser European.

C

Chache, few.
* Chafu, dirt, dirty.
Chagua Ku-, to choose, to select.
* Chai, tea.
Chaki, chalk, whitening, putty.
* Chakula, food, a meal.
Chandarua, tarpaulin, mosquito
net.
Changanya Ku-, to mix.
Chanja Ku-, to inoculate.
Chanjiwa Ku-, to be inoculated.
* Cheka Ku-, to laugh.
* Chelewa Ku-, to be too late, to
over-sleep.

* Chemuka Ku-, to boil, to bubble
up.
Chemusha Ku-, to cause to boil.
Cheroni, dung, manure.
* Cheza Ku-, to play, to cause to
laugh.
* Chimba Ku-, to dig.
* Chini, on the ground, down, below.
Chinja Ku-, to kill for food, to
slaughter.
* Choka Ku-, to become tired.
Choma Ku, to burn, scorch, scald.
Chonga Ku-, to cut to a point, to
whittle.
* Choo, a latrine, lavatory.
Chooni, in the latrine.
Chora Ku-, to steal.
* Chui, a leopard.
* Chukua, Ku-, to carry, take away.
* Chuma, a tool, iron.
Chumba, a room.
* Chumvi, salt.
Chuna Ku-, to flay, to skin.
* Chunga Ku-, to herd, to tend, to
look after, to keep.
Chunga Ku-, to sift, put through
a sieve.
Chungu, bitter, stinging.
Chungwa, pl., Machungwa, an
orange.
* Chupa, a bottle.
Chura, a frog.

D

Dafrau, a collision.
Dafu, pl., Madafu, a cocoa-nut
for milk.
Dai Ku-, to claim a debt, to sue.
Dakika, a minute, minutes.
Dakitari, a doctor, veterinary
officer.
Damu, blood.
* Danganya Ku-, to cheat.
Daraja, a bridge, step, stair-case.
Darubini, a telescope, binoculars
Dari, a roof, upper story.
Dau, pl., Madau, native sailing
boat, a dhow.
* Dawa, medicine, witchcraft charm,
chemicals, polish.
Dawa Ya Kuhara, a purgative.
Dawa ya Kutapika, an emetic

* Debe, ⊢ kerosine tin, large tin.
* Deni, a debt, debts.
Deraiba = Dereva, a driver.
* Desturi, a custom.
Dira, a compass (magnetic
* Dirisha, a window.
* Dobi, a washerman.
-Dogo, small, little.
* Dudu, an insect.
* Duka, a shop.
Dumu ku-, to capture

E

Ebasha = Bahasha, envelope.
Elfu, a thousand.
Enda Kw-, to go.
Enenda ! go on !
Ewe ! You there ! Hi ! I say, you !

F

Fa Ku-, to die.
Faa Ku-, to be of use to, to be suitable.
* Fagia Ku -, to sweep.
* Fagio = Ufagio, a broom.
Fahamu Ku-, to understand.
Faida, profit, gain.
Fanana Ku-, to become like, to resemble.
Fanti (Mil.) Sir
* Fanya Ku-, to do, to make.
Faraipani, a frying pan.
Farasi, a horse.
* Fereji, channel, drain, ditch, water-furrow, water-pipe.
Fetha, silver, money.
Feza = Fetha.
Ficha Ku-, to hide.
Figo, kidney.
* Fika Ku-, to arrive, to reach.
Fikiri Ku-, to consider, to ponder.
Fimbo, a walking stick.
Firimbi, a whistle, flute, pipe.
Fisi, a hyæna.
Fitina, false witness, slander, sowing of discord, intrigue.
Fito, a long slender stick, a purlin.
Foleni , (Eng.) Fall in ! labour muster.

Frasi, a horse.
Frazla, a weight of thirty-six pounds.
* Fua Ku-, to wash clothes.
* Fuata Ku-, to follow, to obey.
* Fukuza Ku-, to drive away, to chase.
Fulana, knitted jumper, sweater vest.
Fumuka Ku-, to come unsewn.
* Fundi, a skilled workman, an expert.
* Fundisha Ku-, to teach.
Fundo, a knot.
* Funga Ku-, to shut, to fasten, to tie, to bind, to imprison.
* Fungua Ku-, to open, to unfasten, to untie, to undo, to release.
* Funguo, keys.
* Funika Ku-, to cover over.
-Fupi, short.
Furai Ku-, to rejoice, to be glad.
Futa Ku-, to wipe, to discharge a servant.
Futi, piece work, daily task, measurement, a foot length, a tape or yard measure.

G

Gali, dear, expensive.
Ganda, pl., Maganda, husk, rind, shell, bark.
* Gani ? What sort of ? What ? Which ?
Gasia, rubbish, litter.
Garama, expenses, transport charges.
* Gari, wagon, cart, wheeled vehicle.
Gawa Ku-, to divide, to share.
Gazeti, a newspaper.
-Geni, foreign, strange
Gereza, prison, gaol
Gerezani, in prison.
Geuka Ku-, to become changed, to turn.
Geuza Ku-, to cause to change, to turn.
Giza or Kiza, darkness.
Godoro, mattress.
Goi-Goi, crooked, worthless, wonky.
Gombana Ku-, to quarrel.

Gombe = Ngombe, cattle, oxen, a cow.
Gonjwa = Mgonjwa, ill.
Goti, *pl.*, Magoti, the knee.
* -Gumu, hard, difficult.
Gunia, a sack, a large bag.
Gurudumo, a wheel.
Guruguru, a turkey.
Gusa Ku-, to touch.

H

* Habari, news, information.
Hadithi, a story, tale, legend.
Haifai ! it won't do ! it's no good !
Haina, it is not.
* Haithuru, it does no harm ! it doesn't matter ! never mind ! all right.
Haizuru = Haithuru.
Haki, justice, right.
   Mutu wa Haki, a fair-minded man.
Hakuna, there is none.
* Halafu, afterwards, presently.
Hali, health, condition.
   U Hali Gani ? how are you ?
   Ni Hali Njema, I am quite well
Hama Ku-, to change house, to move.
* Hamsini, fifty.
Hana, he has not, he has none.
Handaki, a trench.
* Hapa, here.
* Hapana, there is none here, there is none, no, not, none.
* Hara Ku-, to be purged, to have diarrhoea.
* Haribika Ku-, to become destroyed, to be spoilt, to become unusable.
Haribu Ku-, to destroy, to spoil, to put out of action.
Harifu ku-, to inform
Harufu, a smell, a letter of the alphabet
Hasara, loss.
* Hata, until, as far as, even.
Hatari danger
Hatua, a pace, a yard, a footprint
Hawa, these (of animate beings)
Hawezi, he cannot, he is ill.

Haya, these (of Pl. Ma- class).
Haya ! come along ! be quick ! get on with it !
Hema, a tent.
Heri, happy, fortunate.
   Ni Heri, it is better that.
* Kwa Heri, Good-bye.
Hesabu, number, an account.
Hesabu Ku-, to count, to number.
Heshima, honour, reputation
Hewa, air.
* Hii, this, these (normal).
Hiki, this (of Ki- class).
Hili, this (of Ma- class).
Hivi, thus, like this.
Hivi-hivi, in disorder, topsy-turvy.
Hivi, these (of Ki- class).
Hivyo, these things we are talking about (for Ki- class).
Hiyo, this or these that we ar talking about.
Hizi, these (of N- class).
Hodari, strong, capable
* Hodi ? may I come in ?
   Kupiga Hodi, to cry " hodi," to knock on a door, to ask if one may enter another's house.
* Homa, fever, 'flue, a cold.
* Huko, there, over there.
Hukumu ku-, to judge, to pass judgment, to sentence
Hukumu, a sentence, a judgment
Huu, this (of M- class inanimate, and U- class).
Huyu, this (of animate beings).

I

* Iba Kw-, to steal.
* Iko, there is, it is there, is there ?
* Ile, that, those (normal).
Imara, firm, steady.
Imba Kw-, to sing.
Ina, it has, they have.
Inchi, land, country, earth.
* Ine, four.
Ingia Ku-, to enter, to go or come in
* Ingine, other, different, more.
Ini, the liver.
* Inje, outside, out.
Inua Ku-, to lift up, to raise.
Inzi, *pl.*, Mainzi, a fly.

Isha Kw-, to come to an end, to be finished, to finish.

* Ishirini, twenty.

* Ita Kw-, to call, to name.

* Iva Kw-, to become ripe, to get done (*i.e.*, cooked, fermented, etc.).

J

* Jaa Ku-, to become full.

Jamananda, auction, cattle crush.

Jambo, an affair, a matter.

* Jambo ! for Si Jambo, I have no affairs, I am all right ! Hu Jambo ? are you all right ? Ha Jambo ? is he all right ? (hence) greeting ! how d'you do ! Kupata Jambo, to get well.

* Jana, yesterday.

Jangwa, barren land, a desert.

Jani, *pl.*, Majani, a leaf.

* Jaribu Ku-, to try.

Jasho, sweat, perspiration.

* Jaza Ku- = Jasha Ku-, to cause to become filled, to fill.

Jeli, gaol, prison.

* Jembe, a hoe, a plough.

Jembe ya Sahani, a disc plough.

Jembe ya Sungura, a mouldboard plough.

* Jenga Ku-, to build, to construct.

Jeraha, a wound

Jeshi, a great company, an army. Jeshi La Wokovu, Salvation Army.

Jezi, Jeyes Fluid, any disinfectant.

Jibini, cheese.

Jibu Ku-, to answer.

Jicho, *pl.*, Macho, the eye.

Jifu, *pl.*, Majifu or Maivu, ashes.

Jifunza Ku-, to teach oneself, to learn.

* Jiko, a fireplace. *Jikoni, in the kitchen, the kitchen.

* Jina, *pl.*, Majina, a name.

Jino, *pl.*, Meno, a tooth.

* Jioni, evening.

Jipu, a boil, abscess.

Jiwe, *pl.*, Mawe, a stone.

Jogoo, *pl.*, Majogoo, a cock.

Jomba, mother's brother, maternal uncle.

Jora, a thirty-yard piece of Amerikani.

Jozi, a pair, a pack (of cards).

* Jua, the sun.

* Jua Ku-, to know, to know about.

* Juma or Jumaa, Friday, a week.

* Juma Mosi, Saturday.

* Juma Pili, Sunday.

* Juma Tatu, Monday.

* Juma Ine, Tuesday.

* Juma Tano, Wednesday.

* Juu, the top, up, on top, high. Juu ya, above, upon, over, on top of.

* Juzi, the day before yesterday. Juzi-Juzi, a short while ago, the other day.

K

* Kaa Ku-, to stay, to remain, to live at.

* Kabadi, a cupboard.

Kabla, or Kabila, a tribe.

Kabla ya, before (of time).

Kabura, South African Dutch.

Kaburi, a grave

Kadiri, medium, middling

* Kahawa, coffee.

* Kalamu, a pen.

* -Kali, fierce, sharp, cross, acid, strict, savage.

* Kama, if, as, when, like Kama Ku-, to squeeze, to milk.

* Kamata Ku-, to catch, to hold. Kamatana Ku-, to become seized, to solidify, to curdle.

* Kamba, rope, cord, strips of bark used for tying, raw hide thong, a riem.

Kamua Ku-, to squeeze, to milk.

Kando, or Kando-Kando ya, beside, around the outside, at the side of.

Kanga, a guinea-fowl, a native chief's attendant or messenger.

Kanisa, a church.

Kanuni, regulations, written orders

Kanyaga Ku-, to trample, tread on

Kanzu, a long garment like a night-shirt worn by native men.

* Karai, a metal basin, a prospecting pan.

Karanga Ku-, to fry.
Karani, a manager, a secretary, a clerk.
Karata, playing cards.
* Karatasi, paper.
* Karibu, near, soon, close to.
Karutu, a recruit
Kasa, less by
Mbili Kasa Robo, two less by a quarter, *i.e.* one & three quarters
Kasirika-Ku, to be angry.
Kaskazini, north
* Kataa Ku-, to refuse.
* Kata Ku-, to cut.
Kátika = Katka, at, from, in, by (etc.).
Katika Ku-, to come to pieces, to be broken, to be cut.
* Kati-Kati, in the middle, between, amidst.
* Katka = Kátika, at, in (etc.).
* Kauka Ku-, to get dry, to dry up.
-Kavu, dry, dessicated.
Kaza Ku-, to fix, to tighten.
* Kazi, work, business, employment.
* Kelele, noise, row, uproar, shut up !
* Kengele, a bell.
* Kesho, to-morrow.
Kesho Kutwa, the day after to-morrow.
Kesi, a law case.
Kesikei, skey, wooden side pieces through ox-yoke.
* Keti Ku-, to sit down, to stay, to stay at home and do no work.
Keyaa, the K.A.R. regiment, the army
Kiatu, *pl.*, Viatu, shoe, boot, sandal.
Kiazi, *pl.*, Viazi, a sweet potato, a potato.
* Kibaba, a measure of capacity, a tin for measuring. Kibaba ya Posho, about 2½lbs. of maize meal, a tin for measuring the same (usually a 1lb. tea tin).
Kibanda, a shed, a hut.
* Kiberiti, a box of matches, sulphur.

* Kiboko, a hippopotamus-hide whip, a raw-hide whip, a hippopotamus.
Kibuyu, a gourd, calabash, the fruit of the Mbuyu or baobab tree.
Kichungo, a sieve.
* Kichwa, a head.
Kidevu, the chin.
* Kidogo, a little, a small piece, small, little, few, young, the lesser. Kidogo-Kidogo, little by little, by degrees.
* Kidole, a finger, a toe.
Kidonda, a sore place, a wound.
Kifaru, a rhinoceros.
* Kifua, the chest, lungs.
Kifuko, a small bag, pocket, purse.
Kifungo, a button, a fastener.
Kifuniko, a lid, a cover.
Kigingi, tent peg, peg.
Kiingereza, English
Kijana, a youth, a young one. immature.
Kijiji, a village.
Kijiko, a spoon.
* Kikapu, a basket.
Kiko, a tobacco pipe.
Kikoi, a white cloth with coloured border.
* Kikombe, a cup.
* Kila, each, every.
Kilima, a hill.
Kilindi, deep water.
Kima, a monkey.
* Kimbia Ku-, to run, to run away
Kinanda, a musical instrument, piano, mouth organ, gramophone.
Kinwa, a mouth.
Kioga, *pl.*, Vioga, mushroom.
Kiongozi, a guide.
Kioo, a looking-glass, a window pane.
* Kipande, native registration certificate, a piece, a slice.
Kipele, a pimple.
Kipini, a nob, a handle.
Kiranda = Kiwanda.
Kiroboto, a flea.

Kisahani, a saucer, a small plate..
Kisha, afterwards, next.
Kishenzi, barbarous, make-shift.
Kisibau, a waist-coat.
Kisigino, elbow, heel
Kisima, a well.
Kisiwa, an island.
Kisonono, gonorrhea.
* **Kisu,** a knife.
* **Kitabu,** a book.
* **Kitambaa,** a cloth, a rag, a duster, a towel, a curtain, a bed-spread, any cloth stuff other than clothing.
* **Kitanda,** a bedstead, a stand made of rough timber to keep things off the ground, an erection on legs to shade seed beds.
* **Kiti,** a chair, a stool.
* **Kitu,** a thing.
   Kila Kitu, everything.
   Hapana Kitu, nothing.
Kitunguu, *pl.*, **Vitunguu,** an onion
Kiu, thirst.
Kiungwana, in a civilised way.
Kivuko, a ford.
Kivulini, in the shade.
Kiwanda, an enclosed yard, cattle crush, cattle auction.
Kizibo, a cork, a stopper.
Kizungu, European.
Kodi, Government tax.
* **Kofia,** cap, hat.
* **Kohoa Ku-,** to cough.
Kojoa ku-, to urinate
Komaa Ku-, to be full grown.
Konda Ku-, to become thin.
* **Kondoro,** a sheep.
Kongoni, a hartebeest.
Kopa Ku-, to borrow.
Kopesha Ku- or **Kopeza,** to lend.
Korokoroni (Mil.) a prisoner's cell.
Koroga Ku-, to stir.
Koru = **Nkulu,** a waterbuck.
* **Kosa Ku-,** to be at fault, to blunder, to be wrong, to miss.
* **Kosa,** (*pl.*) **Makosa,** a fault, mistake, an entry on conduct sheet (Mil.)
* **Kubali Ku-,** to accept, to agree to.

* **Kubwa,** great, large, important.
   Kichwa   Kubwa, swollenheaded, impertinent.
* **Kufa,** to die.
* **Kufuli,** a padlock.
* **Kuja,** to come.
* **Kuku,** a fowl, poultry.
-**Kukuu,** worn out, old.
* **Kula,** to eat, to drink.
Kule, over there, far off.
Kulia, on the right.
Kuliko, than.
Kumbi-Kumbi, flying white ants (eaten alive).
Kumbuka Ku-, to remember.
Kumbusha Ku-, to remind.
* **Kumi,** ten.
Kunde, beans.
* **Kuni,** firewood.
Kunguni, bed-bug.
Kunja Ku-, to fold.
Kunywa, to drink, to suck up.
* **Kupa,** to give.
Kusanya Ku-, to gather, to collect.
Kushoto, on the left.
Kusini, south.
Kutana Ku-, to meet.
Kutu, rust.
-**Kuu,** great, chief.
   Siku Kuu, Christmas, birthday.
Kuume, on the right.
Kuwa, to become, to be.
Kuwa na, to be with, to have.
Kuza = **Kuuza,** to sell.
* **Kwa,** by means of, to a person (also used in place of Katika).
* **Kwake,** to him or her, to his house, at his house.
* **Kwako,** to you, to your house, at your house.
Kwama Ku-, to be stuck in the mud.
Kwamba, that, if, though.
* **Kwangu,** to me, to my house, at my house.
* **Kwanza,** at first, to start with, first.
Kwao, to them, to'or'at their house.
* **Kweli,** true, the truth.
* **Kwenda,** to go, to go away.
Kwenu, *pl.*, to you, to or at your house.

Kwetu, to us, to or at our house.
Kwiba, to steal.
Kwita, to call out, to call by name.
* **Kwisha,** finished, to end.
Kwiva, to become ripe, to get done.
Kwota gaad, guardroom

L

La Ku- = Kula, to eat, consume, use up.
* **Labda = Labuda,** perhaps.
Laini, a line, barracks
Laini, soft, smooth, pliable.
* **Lakini,** but, however.
* **Lala Ku-,** to sleep, to lie down.
* **Lazma,** it is necessary to, must.
Legea Ku-, to be loose, slack.
Legeza Ku-, to loosen.
Lenge-Lenge, a blister.
* **Leo,** to-day.
Leso, a form of dress for native women.
Leta Ku-, to bring, to fetch.
* **Letea Ku-,** to bring to or for someone.
Lewa Ku-, to become drunk.
* **Lia Ku-,** to weep, mourn, make a fuss about, cry out, shout, make its sound or call.
* **Lima Ku-,** to cultivate, to hoe, to plough.
Limao, a lemon.
Linda Ku-, to guard, to defend
Linga Ku-, to aim a gun
Lini ? when ?
* **Lipa Ku-,** to pay (a debt).
Lipia Ku-, to pay (a person).
Lisha Ku-, to feed.
Liwali, a Swahili chief or governor.
Loboti, report, news.
Lokota Ku- = Kuokota, to pick up.
Lozi, an almond.

M

Maana, meaning, reason, cause
Mabata, ducks, geese
* **Mabati,** corrugated iron, tin sheeting.

Mabega, shoulders.
Mabeti, ammunition pouches.
Mabusu, (Mil.) a prisoner, an accused
Machera, a stretcher.
Machezo, a game.
* **Macho,** eyes. **Macho Ine,** a man who wears glasses.
Machungwa, oranges.
Madoadoa, spotted, mottled, piebald.
* **Mafuta,** oil, fat, petrol.
Mafuta ya Uto, simsim oil.
Mafuta ya Taa, paraffin.
Magadi, coarse soda.
Maganda, peel, rind, bark, husk, cartridge case.
Magoti, knee, knees.
Mahali, place, site.
Mahali Pa or **ya,** instead of
* **Maharagwe,** beans.
* **Mahindi,** maize, Indian corn.
* **Majani,** grass, leaves.
Rangi ya Majani, green.
* **Maji,** water, juice, liquid.
Maji Maji, wet.
Majibu, an answer.
Majivu, burnt-out ashes.
Makaa, embers, cinders, coals.
Makaa ya Miti, charcoal.
Makasi, scissors, pliers.
Makindu, a palm used for making baskets.
Makonge, sisal.
Makorofi, untrained, wild (of oxen), malignant.
Makosa, fault, mistakes, error, crime.
Maktab (Mil.) orderly room
Makumbi, cocoa-nut fibre.
Makusudi, on purpose, intentionally.
Malaya, unfertile, barren, a harlot.
Makuyu, a wild fig tree
* **Mali,** goods, property, riches.
Malimau, lemons.
* **Maliza Ku-,** to complete, to finish.
Malozi, almonds.
* **Mama,** mother.
Mama Kidogo, stepmother, aunt.

Mamba, crocodile, a species of snake.

Mananasi, pineapples.

Maneno, words, language, message, business, argument, affair.

Mangaribi, west.

Manowari, man-of-war, warship.

Manyata, a Masai homestead.

Maongo = Mukongo, the back, loins.

Mapatano, an agreement.

Mapema, early.

Mapenzi, affection, pleasure, love.

Mapigano, a fight, a battle.

Mapumbo, testicles.

* Mara, a time.
* Mara Moja, once, at once, immediately.

Mara ya Mosi, the first time.

Mara Mbili, twice.

Mara Ingine, another time, again,oncemore, some other time

Mara Nyingi, often.

Mara Kwa Mara, from time to time.

* Maridadi, a dandy, smartly dressed, smart, good tone, highly coloured.

Mashariki, east.

Maskini, poor, a poor person, a beggar.

* Masikio, ears, an ear.

Matamayo, a wild olive tree.

Matamu, sweet.

Matandiko, harness, saddle, accoutrements.

Matata, trouble, embroilment.

Mate, spittle.

Matiti, tits, udder, breasts.

* Matofali, bricks.

Matope, mud.

* Matunda, fruit.

Maua, flowers.

Mavi, dung, droppings, manure.

Mavuno, harvest, picking, reaping.

* Mawe, stone, stones, gravel, hail.
* Mayai, eggs.
* Maziwa, milk.
* Mbali, far, distant, separate.

Mbasha, a corporal.

Mbau, boards, shelves, planking.

Mbavu, ribs.

* Mbaya, bad

Mbegu, seed, seeds.

* Mbele, before, in front, further on

Mbichi, raw, unripe, green, underdone.

* Mbili, two. Mbili Mbili, two by two, in pairs.

Mbio, Kupiga Mbio, to run, to gallop.

Mbivu, ripe, well-done.

* Mboga, vegetables.

Mbogo, buffalo.

* Mbovu, rotten, over-ripe, bad.

Mbu, mosquito.

Mbugani, open country.

Mbuni, an ostrich.

Mbuyu, a baobab tree.

* Mbuzi, a goat.
* 'Mbwa, a dog, jackal.

Mchafu, dirt, dirty.

Mchana, daytime, daylight.

* Mchanga, sand, earth.

Mchawi, a witch-doctor.

* Mchele, rice.

Mchezo, a game.

Mchunga or Mchungi, a herdsman.

Mdogo, small, young, the lesser.

Mdomo, the lips.

Meli, a steam-ship, mail steamer, mail.

* Memsaab, a European woman or girl.
* Meno, teeth, a tooth.
* Meza, a table.

Mfalme, King

Mfuko, a bag, a pocket.

Mfupa, a bone.

* Mfupi, short, low.

Mganga, doctor, diviner.

* Mgeni, a stranger, a guest, a foreigner.
* Mgonjwa, a sick person, ill, diseased.
* Mia, a hundred.

Miba, thorns.

Michache, few.

* Midomo, the lips.

Miezi, months.

Mifupa, bones.

* Miguu, legs, feet, wheels

Mikebe, small tins.

Mikono, hands, arms.

Mikuke, spears, a spear.

Milango, doors, a door, a native chief's messenger, an under chief.

Milima, hills, a hill, a mountain, an ant-hill.

Mimba, pregnancy, pregnant.

* Mimi, I, me.

* Mingi, many, much.

Mistari, lines.

Misumari, nails.

Mitalimbo, a crow-bar, an iron bar

Mitego, traps, a trap.

* Miti, trees, a tree, a stick, wood, a pole, sticks, poles, bushes.
Ya Miti, wooden, made of wood.

Miwa, sugar-canes.

Mizabibu, raisins, currants, grapes.

Mizani, weighing machines, scales.

* Mizigo, loads (of 60lbs.), bundles, packages, something to be carried.

Mizizi, roots.

Mji, a town

Mjinga, a fool, an ignorant person.

Mjomba, maternal uncle.

Mkale, fierce, strict, angry, sharp.

* Mkate, bread, a loaf.

Mke, a female, a wife.

* Mkebe, a tin (small).

Mkeka, a grass mat.

Mkia, a tail.

Mkoba, a haversack

Mkondo, a dry river bed

* Mkono, a hand, an arm.

Mkristo, a Christian.

* Mkubwa, large, great, important, the eldest, big.

Mkuke, a spear.

* Mlango = Milango, door, lesser chief.

* Mlima = Milima, a mountain, hill.

Mlingote, a mast, a waggon pole, flag-pole.

Mlinzi, a guard, sentry.

Mlio, a call

Mnada, an auction.

* Moja, one.

Moja Moja, one by one.

* Moshi, smoke, steam.

Ya Mosi, first.

* Moto, fire.
Ya Moto, hot.

Moyo, heart, mind, will.

Mpagazi, a caravan-porter, a workman.

Mpaka, a boundary, until, as far as.

* Mpira, india-rubber, a ball, a tyre, anything made of india-rubber.

* Mpishi, a cook.

Mpunga, unpolished rice

* 'Mpya, new.

* Mrefu, long, tall, high.

Msaada, reinforcements, help.

* Mshahara, monthly pay, wages.

Mshale, an arrow.

Msharage, a hard-wood tree

Msharidi, a whip.

Mshenzi, barbarous, uncivilised, bad mannered, backward.

* Mshipi, a belt, a strap.

Mshumaa, a candle.

Msitu = Musito, a forest.

Msumari, a nail.

Msumeno, a saw.

Mtaa, a native homestead

Mtalimbo, a crow-bar.

Mtama, millet, kaffir-corn.

Mtamba, a heifer.

Mtambo, a spring, a spring-trap, an engine

Mtaragwa, a cedar tree

Mtego, a trap.

Mto = Muto, a pillow, a river.

* Mtoni, at the river, a river.

* Mtoto, a child, a young one.

'Mtu = Mutu, a person, somebody, a man.

Mtumbwi, a canoe.

Mtumishi, a servant.

Mtungi, a water jar, earthenware pot.

* Muchawi, a witch-doctor, a rain-maker.

Muchora, a thief.

Mugoi-Goi, a worthless fellow, weakling.

* Muhindi, an Indian.

E

* Muke = Mke, female, feminine.
Mukongo, the back, lumbar regions.
* Mume, male, masculine.
Mulevi, a drunkard.
* Mungu, God.
Shauri ya Mungu, fate, kismet
* Muto, a pillow, a cushion, a mattress.
* Mutu, a person, somebody, a human being.
Mvita, Mombasa island.
Mviringo, circumference, circle.
Mvivu, idle, lazy.
* Mvua, rain.
* Mwaga Ku-, to pour away, empty out, spill.
Mwagika Ku-, to become spilt, emptied out.
* Mwaka, a year.
Mwalimu, a teacher.
Mwamba, a rock
Mwana, a son, a child.
* Mwana Muke, a woman, a female.
Mwana Mume, a male.
Mwanzi, a bamboo.
Mwanzo, the beginning.
Mwashi, a mason, a stone-worker.
Mwavuli, an umbrella, sun-shade.
Mwema, good.
Mwembamba, narrow, thin.
Mwembe, a mango.
* Mwenyewe, the owner, self.
Mwenyi, having, possessing.
* Mwenzi, a companion.
Mweupe, white, light coloured.
Mweusi, a black man, black, dark coloured.
* Mwezi, the moon, a month.
Mwiba, a thorn.
Mwiko, a spoon (large), a trowel.
* Mwili, the body.
* Mwisho, the end.
Ya Mwisho, the last, the end one.
Mwislamu, a Mahommedan.
Mwitu, forest
Mwivi, a thief.
Mwoga, a coward.
* Mzee, an old person, old, aged.

Mzigo, a load, a bundle, a package.
* Mzima, a healthy man, healthy, whole, complete, the whole.
Mzinga, a cannon.
* Mzungu, a European, a white man.
* Mzuri, good, beautiful, excellent, fine.

N

* Na, and, also, by, with.
Nafasi, time, opportunity, space, room.
Nami, with me.
Namna, sort, pattern.
* Namna Gani ? of what sort ? in what way ?
* Namna Hii, in this way, like this
* Nane, eight.
* Nani ? who ?
Nao, with them.
Nawa Ku-, to wash oneself.
Kunawa Mikono, to wash the hands.
Nayo, with it.
Nazi, a cocoa-nut (fully ripe).
Ndama, a calf.
* Ndani, in, inside, within.
* Ndege, bird, aeroplane.
Nderobo, a forest dweller, forest tribe.
* Ndio, it is so, yes.
Ndimu, lime juice, lemon.
* Ndito, an unmarried girl.
* Ndizi, bananas.
* Ndoo, a bucket.
Ndovu, an elephant.
* Ndugu, a brother or sister, a cousin, a relation, a friend.
Ndui, smallpox.
Ndume, a male animal.
Nena Ku-, to speak.
Nene, thick, wide, stout.
Neno, pl., Maneno, a word.
Neopara, a foreman, head-man.
Neupe = Nyeupe, white, light coloured.
Neusi = Nyeusi, black, dark coloured
* Ngambo, the opposite bank, the other side of a valley.

Ngamia, a camel.
Ngano, wheat.
Ngapi? how many? how much?
Ngazi, a ladder.
Ngine = Ingine, other, another, different.
Ngoa Ku-, to root up, to pull up by the roots.
Ngoja Ku-, to wait, to wait for.
Ngoma, a dance, a drum.
Ngombe, cattle, a cow, an ox.
Ngozi, a skin, leather, skin.
Ngumu, hard, difficult.
Nguo, clothes, clothing material.
Nguruwe, a pig, warthog.
Nguvu, strength, force, power.
Nguzo, a tent pole, pillar.
Ni, I am, is, was, are, were.
Nimeleti, lemonade.
Nina, I have.
Ninayo, I have it, or them.
Nini? what?
    Kwa Nini? what for? why?
    Ya Nini? for what?
Ninyi, you (pl.).
Ninyi Nyote, all of you.
Nipa, give me (often wrongly used for other persons, i.e., give him).
Njaa, hunger, famine.
'Nje = Inje, outside, out.
Njema, good, very well.
Njia, a path, a way, a road.
Njoo! come!
Njooni! come ye! come all of you!
Njugu, ground nuts, monkey nuts.
Nkulu, water-buck.
'Nne = Ine, four.
Nona Ku-, to get fat.
Nuka Ku-, to be smelly, to stink.
Nundu, a hump, a bullock's hump.
Nungu, a porcupine.
Nunua Ku-, to buy.
Nuru, light, illumination.
Nusa Ku-, to smell something.
Nusu or Nus, half, half a rupee, one shilling.
Nyama, animals, meat, flesh.
Nyamaza Ku-, to stop talking, be silent.
Nyangau, a hyaena.
Nyani, a baboon, ape.

Nyanya, a tomato, a monkey.
Nyapara, a foreman, head-man
Nyasi, grass, reeds.
Nyekundu, red.
Nyembamba, thin.
Nyeupe, white, light-coloured.
Nyeusi, black, dark-coloured.
Nyika, wilderness, desert.
Nyima Ku-, to withhold, to refuse to give.
Nyingi, many, much.
Nyingine, other, different.
Nyoa Ku-, to shave
Nyoka, a snake.
Nyonya Ku-, to suck.
Nyororo, a chain, trek-chain.
Nyorosa Ku-, to stretch.
Nyosha Ku-, to straighten.
Nyota, a star
Nyuki, a bee.
Nyuma, behind, at the back, afterwards.
Nyumba, a house.
Nyumbu, a mule.
Nyundo, a hammer.
Nywa Ku-, to drink, suck up.
Nzige, a locust, locusts.
Nzima, whole, complete, sound.
Nzito, heavy
Nzuri, fine, good, excellent.

O

Oa Ku-, to marry a wife.
Oga Ku-, to bathe, to take a bath.
Ogelea Ku-, to swim.
Ogopa Ku-, to fear, to be afraid.
Oka Ku-, to bake, to roast.
Okota Ku-, to pick up.
Olewa Ku-, to be married to a husband.
Omba Ku-, to pray to, to beg of, to ask for.
Ona Ku-, to see, to perceive, to find, to feel.
Ondoa Ku-, to take away.
Ondoka Ku-, to get up, to go away, to start off.
Onekana Ku-, to appear, to become visible.

* **Ongeza Ku-,** to augment, increase.
* **Onyesha Ku-,** to show, to explain.
* **Oza Ku-,** to go bad, to rot, to decay.

P

Pa Ku-, to give to, *i.e.,* **Nipa** = give me. **'Mpa** = give him. **Wapa** = give them.
* **Paka,** a cat, cats.
* **Pakia Ku-** = **Kubaki,** to remain over.

Pakua Ku, to take food out of the pot, dish up.

Pale, that place, there, just there.

Pamba, cotton, cotton plant, cotton wool.
* **Pamoja,** in one place, together.

Pana, broad, wide.
* **Panda Ku-,** to climb, to ride, to get up on, to plant.
* **Panga,** a sword, a large chopping knife.

Pangusa Ku-, to wipe, to dust.
* **Panya,** a mouse, rat, mole, rodents.

Papayi, *pl.,* **Mapayi,** pawpaws.

Pasha Moto Ku-, to warm up, reheat.
* **Pasi,** a flat-iron, a clothes-iron.
  Kupiga Pasi, to iron clothes.

Pasua Ku-, to split, to rend.
* **Pasuka Ku-,** to become split, to burst, to crack, to explode
* **Pata Ku-,** to get.

Pata, a hinge, hinges

Patasi, a chisel.
* **Peke Yangu,** by myself.
* **Peke Yako,** by yourself.
* **Peke Yake,** by him, her, or itself
* **Peke Yetu,** by ourselves
* **Peke Yenu,** by yourselves.
* **Peke Yao,** by themselves.
* **Peleka Ku-,** to send, to take.

Pelekea Ku-, to send to someone.

Peleleza ku-, to scout
* **Pembe,** a horn, corner, tusk, maize cob.

Pembeni, in the corner.
* **Penda Ku-,** to like, to prefer.

Pendeza Ku-, to please.

* **Pesa,** small change, gold dust, pay.
  Pesa Nane, a quarter of a shilling.

Pewa Ku, to be given
* **Piga Ku-,** to beat, to hit, to strike.

Kupiga Bunduki, to fire a gun.

Kupiga Chapa, to print.

Kupiga Firimbi, to blow a whistle.

Kupiga Fundo, to tie a knot.

Kupiga Hema, to pitch or strike a tent.

Kupiga Hodi, to cry "hodi."

Kupiga Kelele, to make a noise.

Kupiga Kengele, to ring a bell.

Kupiga Kofi, to slap, box the ears.

Kupiga Laini, to draw a line.

Kupiga Loboti, to report, to bring news.

Kupiga Mafoki, to clap the hands.

Kupiga Mbio, to run, to gallop.

Kupiga Mvua, to rain.

Kupiga Ngoma, to beat a drum, to dance.

Kupiga Ngumi, to box

Kupiga Pasi, to iron clothes.

Kupiga Peksen, to inspect.

Kupiga Randa, to use a carpenter's plane.

Kupiga Simu, to send a telegram

Kupiga Teke, to kick.
* **Pigana Ku-,** to fight.
* **Pika Ku-,** to cook.
* **Piki-Piki,** a motor bicycle.

Piksha, a picture, photograph, camera.

Pili, second, number two.
* **Pili-Pili,** pepper.
* **Pima Ku-,** to measure, to weigh.
* **Pindua Ku-,** to overturn, to turn round.

Pinduka Ku-, to be upset, to be turned.

Pini, a safety-pin.

Pipa, *pl.,* **Mapipa,** a barrel, cask.

Pirimbi = **Firimbi,** flute, whistle.

Pishi = **Mpishi,** a cook.
* **Pita Ku-,** to pass, to overtake.
* **Pole-Pole,** slowly, gently.

Pombe, native beer.

Pona Ku-, to get well, to be cured.

Porini, out in the bush, in the rough, bush country.

Posta, post office.

* **Posho,** maize-flour, rations.

* **Potea Ku-,** to become lost.

Poteza Ku-, to cause to become lost, to lose.

Pua, the nose.

Pumbafu, a fool, idiot.

Pumua Ku-, to breathe.

Pumuzi, breath, air.

Pumzika Ku-, to pause for breath, to rest.

* **Punda,** a donkey.

Punda Milia, a zebra.

Punguka Ku-, to become less, to dwindle.

* **Punguza Ku-,** to make less, to reduce.

Pwani, on the beach, the shore.

R

* **Rafiki,** a friend.

Rahisi, cheap, easy.

Raiya -a, civilian

Randa, a carpenter's plane.

Kupiga Randa, to plane a board.

* **Rangi,** colour, paint, dye, varnish, stain.

* **Ratili,** a pound weight, a weighing machine.

-Refu, long, tall.

Rege-Rege, a hand-mill, hand turned machinery.

* **Risasi,** lead, a cartridge, a bullet, a shell

* **Robo,** a quarter.

Kasa Robo, less by a quarter, three quarters.

Roho, conscience, soul, life, will.

* **Rudi Ku-,** to return, to go back, to come back.

* **Rudisha Ku-,** to give back, to send back.

* **Ruka Ku-,** to jump, fly.

Ruksa = Ruhusa, leave, permission, liberty.

* **Rungu,** a club, a cudgel.

Rupia, a rupee, two shillings, money.

S

* **Saa,** hour, clock, watch, o'clock.

* **Saba,** seven.

* **Sababu,** cause, reason, because, why?

* **Sabaini,** seventy.

* **Sabuni,** soap.

Sadiki Ku-, to believe.

* **Safari,** a journey, trip, expedition.

* **Safi,** clean, pure.

* **Safisha Ku-,** to make clean.

* **Saga Ku-,** to grind.

* **Sahani,** a dish, a plate, a disk

* **Sahau Ku-,** to forget.

* **Saidia Ku-,** to help.

Sais, a syce, groom.

Saladi, salad, lettuce.

Salala, sirloin, saddle of meat.

Salamu, greetings, safety.

* **Samaki,** a fish, fish.

Samawi, Rangi ya, blue, sky blue.

Samehe Ku-, to forgive, to overlook a fault.

Samli, ghee, clarified butter.

* **Sana,** very, much (it intensifies any word).

* **Sanduku,** a box.

Sangari, couch grass.

Sangura, a hare, rabbit, hyrax.

* **Sasa,** now.

* **Sasa Hivi,** directly, immediately.

Sauti, voice, noise, sound.

* **Sawa-Sawa,** like, alike, the same, equal, even, level, smooth, correctly.

Sebuleni, in the sitting-room, the parlour.

* **Sema Ku-,** to say, talk, speak.

Sema Sana! speak up! talk louder.

Semeji = Shemegi, brother or sister-in-law.

Sengenge, wire.

Sengenge ya miba, barbed wire

Senti, cent, washer.

* **Serikali,** the government, the law.

Sermala, a carpenter.

Shaba, brass

Shabaha, a rifle range

* **Shamba,** a farm, cultivated land, garden.

Shambulia Ku-, to attack

Shangazi, an aunt.

*Shauri, a matter, business, negotiation, affair, dispute.

Shawesh, a sergeant

Shemeji, brother or sister-in-law.

Shenzi, barbarous, uncivilised, native, unrefined, makeshift.

Shetani = Shaitani, Satan, a devil.

Shiba Ku-, to be full with eating.

Shika Ku-, to hold fast, to lay hold of.

Shilingi, shillings, money.

*Shimo, a pit, excavation, mine, hole.

*Shinda Ku-, to conquer, to get the better of, to defeat, to be better than.

Shindilia Ku-, to ram home, to compress a spring

Shingo, the neck.

*Shoka, an axe, a chopper.

*Shona Ku-, to sew.

Shtaki Ku-, to accuse, prosecute, charge.

Shuka, a sheet, a length of cloth.

Shuka Ku-, to descend, to get off or out of.

*Si, not, is not, are not.

Siafu, a safari ant.

*Siagi, butter.

Sibana, a span or team of oxen.

Sibia Ku- = Kuzuia, to hinder, prevent.

*Sigara, cigarette.

Siki, vinegar.

*Sikia Ku-, to hear, understand. feel, obey.

Sikiliza Ku-, to listen.

Sikio, pl., Masikio, the ears.

*Siku, a day.

Siku Kuu, the great day, Christmas, a birthday.

* Siku Zote, always.

Sikulu, school.

Silaha, a weapon

*Simama Ku-, to stand up, halt, to be upright.

Simamisha Ku-, to cause to stand, to put upright.

*Simba, a lion.

Simu, electric telegraph.

Sina, I have not.

Sinayo, I have none.

* Sindano, needle, thorn

Singe, a bayonet

Sirika ku-, =Kukasirika.

Sirupu, strop, a twisted leather thong joining skeys under neck of yoked ox.

*Sisi, we, us.

Sisi Sote, all of us.

*Sita, six.

*Sitaki, I do not want.

Siti, sheet.

Sitima, electricity, tractor, steam engine.

*Siwezi, I can not, I am not well.

Siyo ! no !

Soko, the market.

Sokota, ku-, to twist

*Soma Ku-, to read, to read the Bible.

Songa, ku-, to close in, press

*Sufuria, a metal cooking pot, a sauce-pan.

Sugua Ku-, to rub, scrub, scour.

*Sukari, sugar.

*Sukuma Ku-, to push.

Sultani, a village head-man, a lesser chief.

Sumbua Ku-, to worry, annoy, give trouble.

Sumu, poison.

*Sumuni, sixpence, fifty cents.

Sungura = Sangura, hare, hyrax, squirrel.

Sururu, a pick-axe.

*Suruali, trousers, shorts, pants.

*Swara, small antelope, oribi, reed-buck.

T

*Taa, a lamp.

Tafathali, (seldom heard) if you please.

*Tafuta Ku-, to look for, search for, seek.

Tahiri Ku-, to become circumcised.

*Taka Ku-, to want.

Tamaam, roll call, "all correct"

-Tamu, sweet, pleasant, good.

Tandarua, tarpaulin, mosquito net

Tandika Ku-, to spread, to saddle, to lay out, to put on the accessories.

* Tangu, since, from.
Tangu Lini ? since when ? for how long ?

Tangulia Ku-, to go first, to precede.

* Tano, five.

Tapika Ku-, to vomit.

Tapua Ku- = Kutoboa, to bore a hole.

Taratibu, gently, carefully, slowly.

Tarehe, the day of the month

Tarimbo = Mtalimbo.

Tasa, a barren animal.

Tatu, three.

Tauni, plague, cholera.

Tayari, ready.

Tazama Ku-, to look.

Tegemea, Ku-, to lean upon

Tego, syphilis.

Tele, plenty, much.

* Tembea Ku-, to walk, go for a walk, wander.

* Tembo, native beer, alcohol, an elephant.

* Tena, afterwards, again, also further.

Tende, dates

* Tengeneza Ku-, to prepare, to make ready, to put to rights, to repair.

Tepe, (Mil.) an N.C.O. stripe

Teremuka Ku-, to go down-hill.

Terensi, trance, a leather thong fastening the trek chain to ox-yoke.

Tetemeka Ku-, to shiver, to tremble.

* Thani Ku- = Kuzani, to think, suppose.

Thelathini, thirty.

* Themanini = Thamanini, eighty.

* Thenashara, (Arabic) twelve. Saa Thenashara, six o'clock.

Thuru Ku-, to harm, injure.
Haithuru, it does not harm, no matter.

Tia Ku-, to put.

* Tiga = Twiga, a giraffe.

Tii Ku-, to oboy.

Tikisa Ku-, te shake, shake out.

Tindo, a stone chisel, cold chisel.

Tinikata, a tin-cutter, tin opener.

Tinka-Tinka, power-driven machinery.

* Tisa, nine.

Titi, nipple, breast, udder.

* Toa Ku-, to take off, give out, put out, take away.

Toboa Ku-, to bore a hole, break through.

Toboka Ku-, to be punctured, be holed.

* Toka Ku-, to come or go out or away from.

* Tope pl., Matope, mud.

Topi, a kind of antelope, topi.

* Toroka Ku-, to run away from a master, to run away.

* Tosha Ku-, to suffice, to be enough.

Tu, only, just, merely, nothing but.

Tukana, Ku-, to abuse, swear at.

Tumaini Ku-, to hope, expect.

Tuma Ku-, to send off on a job, to detail, to employ.

Tumbaku, tobacco, snuff.

* Tumbo, stomach, bowels, womb, insides.

* Tumia Ku-, to use, to spend, to use up.

Tupa, a file.

* Tupa Ku-, to throw.

Tupu, empty, bare, plain, naked.

Tuta pl., Matuta, raised flower bed.

Twiga, a giraffe.

U

* Ua Ku-, to kill.

Ua, pl., Maua, a flower.

Ubau, a plank, board.

Uchafu, filthiness, dirt.

Uchawi, witchcraft.

Uchungu, bitterness, pain.

* Udongo, puddled clay or earth

Ufagio, a broom.

Ufunguo, a key.

* Ugali, porridge, a paste of cooked Posho.

Ugonjwa, illness, sickness, disease.

Ujao, it which is to come
Mwaka ujao, next year. '

* Uji, gruel, a soup of cooked Posho.

Ukelele, a cry, a noise.

Ukarasa, the page of a book.

Ukuta, a stone wall.

* Ulaya, Europe.
Ya Ulaya, from Europe, pedigree, superior.

Ule, that, yonder.

Ulimi, pl., Ndimi, the tongue.

* Uliza Ku-, to question, to ask.

* Uma, a fork, a sting.

* Uma Ku-, to bite, to sting, to pain, ache.

Umande, dew, morning mist.

Umbwa = Mbwa, a dog, jackal.

Umeme, lightning.

Umia Ku-, to give pain to.

Umiza Ku-, to hurt.

Una, you have.

Unayo or Unazo, you have it, you have them.

Unene, thickness.

* Unga, flour, meal.
Ungua Ku-, to catch fire, be scorched.

Upana, breadth, width.

Upande, a side.

Upanga = Panga, a sword, a chopping knife.

Upeo wa macho, the horizon

Upepo, the wind.

* Upesi, quickly, quick.
Upindi, a bow (for arrows).

Upolini = Porini, in the bush, in the rough.

Upumbafu, folly, foolishness.

Upuzi, nonsense.

Urefu, length, height.

* Urongo = Uwongo, a lie, a falsehood.

Ushanga, pl., Shanga, beads.

Ushuru, tax, customs duties.

* Usiku, night, darkness.
Uso, pl., Nyuso, a face.

Uta, Mafuta ya, simsim oil.

Utambi, pl., Tambi, a lampwick.

Utupu, nakedness, naked.

Uvivu, idleness, laziness.

Uvumbi, dust.

Uwongo = Urongo, a lie, a falsehood.

* Uza Ku- = Kuza, to sell.

Uzee, old age.

* Uzi, thread, string, sacking twine.

V

Vaa Ku-, to put on clothes, to dress in.

* Viatu, boots, shoes, sandals.

* Viazi, potatoes.

Vidole, fingers, toes.

Vijiko, spoons.

Vile, those, yonder.

Vile-Vile, just those, like that, the same.

Vimba Ku-, to swell.

* Vioga, mushrooms, edible food.

Vipele, pimples, a rash.

Vishakani, open bush country

Visikoro, the cores of maize cobs.

Vita, war

Vitu, things.

* Vitunguu, onions.

* -Vivu, idle, lazy.

Vizuri, fine, well, excellently.

* Vumbi, pl., Mavumbi, dust.

Vuna Ku-, to reap, gather the harvest.

Vunja Ku-, to break.

* Vunjika Ku-, to become broken.

* Vuta Ku-, to pull.

W

Wa, of.

Wa Ku-, to be, to become.

* Wacha Ku- = Kuacha, to allow, to let, to let go, to leave alone.

* Wacha Maneno, stop talking !

* Wageni, guests, strangers, foreigners.

* Wagonjwa, sick people, invalids.

Wajinga, fools, ignorant people.

Waka Ku-, to blaze, to be alight.

Wakati, time, season, while whilst.

Wake, his, her, its, female.

Wako, thy, thine.

Wale, those, yonder.

Wali, cooked rice.

Wana, they have.
* Wana Wake, women.
Wanaume, menfolk.
Wanderobo, members of a forest tribe.
Wanga, starch, arrowroot.
Wangu, my, mine.
Wao, their.
Wapagazi, caravan porters, workmen.
* Wapi ? where ?
Washa Ku-, to light, to set fire to.
Washenzi, savages, uncivilised people.
* Watoto, children.
* Watu, people, men or women.
Waume, males, men.
Wawile, two, two people.
　Wote Wawili, both.
Waya (Eng.) wire, wire netting.
* Wazee, old people.
Wazi, open, clear.
* Wazungu, Europeans.
* Weka Ku-, to place, to put away. put down.
Wembe, a razor.
Wengi, many.
Wengine = Ingine, (of people), other, different, more.
Wenu, your (plural), yours.
Weupe, white, white people.
* Weusi, black, black people, Africans.
Wevi, pl., of Mwivi, thieves.
* Wewe, thou, thee.
* Weza Ku-, to be able.
Wiki, a week.
Wimbi, millet, eleusine grain.
Winda Ku-, to hunt, to shoot game
Wino, ink.
Wote, all.

Y

* Ya, of.
Yai, pl., Mayai, an egg.

* Yake, his, her, its.
* Yako, thy, thine, your.
* Yangu, my, mine.
Yao, their, theirs.
Yenu, your (plural), yours
* Yetu, our, ours.
* Yeye, him, her.
Yoki, an ox-yoke.
* Yote, all.
Yule, that person, yonder person.

Z

Za, of.
Za Ku- = Kuuza, to sell.
* Zaa Ku-, to give birth, to bear fruit.
* Zaidi, more.
Zake, his, her, its.
Zako, thy, thine.
Zaliwa Ku-, to be born.
Zama Ku-, to sink, to dive.
* Zamani, formerly, long ago, last time.
Zangu, my, mine.
Zani Ku- = Kuthani, to think, suppose.
Zao, their.
Zawadi, a present.
Zenu, your (plural), yours.
Zetu, our, ours.
Zika Ku-, to bury.
Zile, those, yonder.
Zima, ku, to extinguish a light
-Zima, whole, healthy, complete.
-Zito, heavy.
Ziwa, swamp, pond, reservoir, breast.
Zote, all.
Zuia Ku-, to hinder, prevent.
Zulia, a carpet.
Zunguka Ku-, to go round, revolve, wander.
-Zuri, fine, beautiful, handsome.

ENGLISH-SWAHILI VOCABULARY

A

Able, to be, **ku-weza**
Above, **juu**
Absolutely, **kabisa**
Accept, to, **ku-kubali**
Accuse, to, **ku-shtaki**
Affair, **shauri**
After, **baada ya**
Afterwards, **halafu**
Again, **tena**
Agree, to, **ku-patana**
Agreement, **mapatano**
Aim, **shabaha**
Aim, to, **ku-linga**
Alcohol, **tembo**
Alike, **sawa-sawa.**   [people)
All, **yote** (of things), **wote** (of
Also, **na**
Always, **siku zote**
Ammunition, **risasi.**
Ammunition pouches, **mabete**
Among, **kati-kati ya**
And, **na**
Angry, to be. **ku-kasirika.**
Animal, **nyama**
Annoy, to, **ku-sumbua**
Answer, an, **majibu**
Answer, to, **ku-jibu**
Ant (safari), **siafu**
Ant (Termite) white, **Mchwa**, or
    when in edible flying stage
    Kumbi-Kumbi
Appear, to, **ku-onekana**
Arm, **mkono**
Armpit, **kwapa**
Arrange, to, **ku-tengeneza**
Arrive, to, **ku-fika**
Arrow, **mshale**
Artisan, **fundi**
As, **kama**
Ascend, to, **ku-panda**
Ashes, **maivu**
Ask a question, to, **ku-uliza**
Ask for, to, **ku-omba**
At, **katika**
Attack to, **ku-shambulia**
Auction, **mnada, jamananda**
Aunt (maternal), **mama mkubwa,
    mama mdogo**
Aunt (paternal), **shangazi**

Awake, to, **ku-amuka, ku-amusha**
Axe, **shoka**

B

Baboon, **nyani**
Back, of body, **mukongo**
Bad, **mbaya, mbovu**
Badge, a, **Alama**
Bag, **mfuko, gunia**
Bake, to, **ku-oka**
Balance scales, **mizani**
Ball, **mpira**
Banana, **ndizi**
Band of soldiers, **kikozi**
Bank, the opposite, **ngambo**
Baobab tree, **mbuyu**
Barbed wire, **sengenge ya miba**
Bark, of a tree, **maganda**
Barracks, **laini**
Barrel, **pipa**
Barren female, a, **malaya**
Barren land, **jangwa**
Basin (small), **bakuli**
Basket, **kikapu**
Bathe, to, **ku-oga**
Battle, **mapigano**
Bayonet, **singe**
Be, to, **kuwa**
Beads, **ushanga**
Beam, **boriti**
Beans, **maharagwe**
Bear fruit to, **ku-zaa**
Beard, **ndevu**
Beat, to, **ku-piga**
Beautiful, **mzuri**
Because, **kwa sababu, kwa kuwa**
Become, to, **kuwa**
Bedstead, **kitanda**
Bee, **nyuki**
Beer, **pombe, tembo**
Beggar, **maskini**
Before, (of time) **kabla ya**
Begin, to, **ku-anza**
Beginning, **mwanzo**
Behind, **nyuma ya**
Believe, to, **ku-sadiki**
Bell, **kengele**
Below, **chini ya**
Belt, **mshipi**

Bend, to, ku-pindua
Big, mkubwa
Bind, to, ku-funga
Bird, ndege
Birth, to give, ku-zaa
Biscuit, bisikoti
Bite. to, ku-uma
Bitter, chungu
Black, nyeusi
Blank round, a, baruti
Blood, damu
Boards, bau
Boat, mashua
Body, mwili
Boil, to (bubble), ku-chemuka,
„ to put to, ku-chemusha
Bones, mifupa
Book, kitabu
Boots, viatu
Bore a hole, to, ku-toboa
Born, to be, ku-zaliwa
Borrow, to, ku-kopa
Bottle, chupa
Boundary, mpaka
Bow (for arrows), upindi
Bowels, tumbo
Bowl, bakuli
Box, to, ku-piga ngumi
Box, sanduku
Brain, ubongo
Brand, to, ku-choma alama
Brass, shaba
Breadth, upana
Break, to, ku-vunja
Breasts, matiti
Breath, pumuzi
Bricks, matofali
Bridge, daraja
Bring, to, ku-leta
Broad, pana
Broken, to be, ku-vunjika
Broom, ufagio
Brother, ndugu
Brother-in-law, shemeji
Bubble, to ku-chemuka
Buck, a, swara
Bucket, ndoo
Bug, a bed, kunguni
Bugle, a, buruji
Bugle call, a, mlio wa buruji
Bugler, burujee

Buffalo, mbogo
Build, to, ku-jenga
Bullet, risasi
Bundles, mizigo
Burn, to, on purpose, ku-choma
    by accident, ku-ungua
Burst, to, ku-pasuka
Bury, to, ku-zika
Bush-buck, bongo
open Bush Country, vishakani
Bush Country, porini
But, lakini
Butter, siagi
Button, kifungo
Buy, to, ku-nunua
By, kwa

C

Calf, ndama
Call, to, ku-ita
Camera, piksha
Cancel, to, ku-futa
Candle, mshumaa
Canoe, mtumbwi
Cannon, mzinga
Cap, kofia
Capture, to, ku-dumu
Cards, karata
Care, to take, Ku-anglia
Carefully, taratibu
Carry, to, ku-chukua, ku-beba
Cart, gari
Cartridge, S.A.A., risasi
Cartridge case, Arty., maganda
Cat, paka
Catch, to, ku-kamata
Cattle, ngombe
Cattle crush, Jamananja.
Cause, sababu
Cedar tree, mtaragwa
Cell, prison (mil.), korokoroni
Chain, nyororo
Chair, kiti
Chalk, chokaa
Change, to, ku-badili
Charcoal, makaa
Cheap, rahisi
Cheat, to, ku-danganya
Chemicals, dawa
Chest, of body, kifua
Chicken, kuku
Chief, kuu

Chief, a, **chifu**
Child, **mtoto**
Chin, **kidevu**
Chisel, cold steel, **tindo**
Chisel, carpenter's, **patasi**
Choose, to, **ku-chagua**
Chop, to, **ku-chonga**
Christian, **Mkristo**
Church, **kanisa**
Circumcise, to, **ku-tahiri**
Civilian, **ya raiya**
Claim a debt, to, **ku-dai**
Clasp, to, **ku-shika**
Claw, **ukucha**
Clean, **safi**
Cleanse, to, **ku-safisha**
Clerk, **karani**
Climb, to, **ku-panda**
Clock, **saa**
Close, to, **ku-funga**
Close in, to, **ku-songa**
Cloth, **kitambaa**
Clothing, **nguo**
Clouds, **mawingu**
Club, **rungu**
Coat, **koti**
Cob (of maize), **pembe**
Cock, **jogoo**
Cocoa-nut, **nazi**
Cocoa-nut leaves, **makuti**
Coffee, **kahawa**
Coffee, dried cherries, **buni**
Cold, **baridi**
Collect, to, **ku-kusanya**
Collision, **dafurao**
Colour, **rangi**
Comb, **kitana**
Come, to, **kuja**
Come on! **Haya!**
Come back, to, **ku-rudi**
Come from, to, **ku-toka**
Companion, **mwenzi**
Compass, magnetic, **dira**
Conduct, good, **adabu**
Conduct, good, badge, **asanta**
Complete, to, **ku-maliza**
Completely, **kabisa**
Conceal, to, **ku-ficha**
Conquer, to, **ku-shinda**
Consider, to, **ku-fikiri**

Cook, **mpishi**
Cook, to, **ku-pika**
Cooking pot, **sufuria**
Cord, **kamba**
Cordite, **baruti**
Cores of maize cobs, **visikoro**
Cork, **kizibo**
Corporal, a, **kopro, mbasha**
Correctly, **sawa-sawa**
Corrugated iron, **mabati**
Cotton, **pamba**
Cough, to, **ku-kohoa**
Count, to, **ku-hesabu**
Country, a, **inchi**
Couple, a, **jozi**
Cousin, **ndugu**
Cover, a, **kifuniko**
Cover, to, **ku-funika**
Cow, **ngombe**
Coward, **mwoga**
Crooked, **goi-goi**
Crowbar, **mtalimbo**
Cry, to, **ku-lia**
Cultivated land, **shamba**
Cultivate, to, **ku-lima**
Cup, **kikombe**
Cured, to become, **ku-pona**
Currants, **mizabibu**
Curry powder, **binzari**
Cushion, **mto**
Custom, **desturi**
Cut, to, **ku-kata**

D

Dance, a, **ngoma**
Danger, **hatari**
Dark, **nyeusi**
Darkness, **gisa**
Dates, **tende**
Date tree, **mtende**
Dawn, **alfajiri**
Day, **siku**
Day of the month, **tarehe**
Daytime, **mchana**
Debt, **deni**
Deceive, to, **ku-danganya**
Decrease, to, **ku-punguza**
Delay, to, **ku-kawia, ku-chelewa**
Dense, **nene**
Depart, to, **ku-ondoka**
Desert, a, **jangwa**

Destroy, to, **ku-haribu**
Destroyed, to become, **ku-hari-bika**
Detail for a job, to, **ku-tuma**
Devil, **shaitani**
Diarrhœa, to have, **ku-hara**
Die, to, **kufa**
Different, **ingine, mbali**
Dig, to, **ku-chimba**
Dirty, **chafu**
Disease, **ugonjwa**
Dish, **sahani**
Dish up, to, **ku-pakua**
Distant, **mbali**
Ditch, **fereji**
Divide, to, **ku-gawa, ku-gawanya**
Do, to, **ku-fanya**
Doctor, **dakitari**
Dog, **mbwa**
Donkey, **punda**
Door, **mlango**
Down, **chini**
Drag, to, **ku-buruta**
Drain, **fereji**
Dress, **nguo**
Drink, to, **kunwa**
Drive away, to, **ku-fukuza**
Drum, **ngoma**
Drunk, to be, **ku-lewa**
Drunkard, **mlevi**
Drunkenness, **ulevi**
Dry, **kavu**
Dry river bed, a, **mkondo**
Dry up, to, **ku-kauka**
Dry, to put out to, **ku-anika**
Duck, a, **bata**
Dung, **mavi, cheroni**
Dust, **vumbi**
Duster, **kitambaa**
Dynamite, **baruti**
Dysentery, to have, **ku-hara damu**

E

Early, **mapema**
Early morning, **asubuhi**
Ears, **masikio**
Earth, wet, **udongo**
Earth, dry, **mchanga**
East, **mashariki**

Easy, **rahisi**
Eat, to, **kula**
Egg, **yai**, *pl.* **mayai**
Eight, **nane**
Eighth, **thumuni**
Eighty, **thamanini**
Elbow, **kisigino cha mkone**
Elephant, **tembo, ndovu**
Eleven, **kumi na moja**
Empty, **tupu**
End, **mwisho**
Enemy, **adui**
England, **Ungereza**
Enough, to be, **ku-tosha**
Enough! **basi!**
Enter to, **ku-ingia**
Entirely, **kabisa**
Entry in Conduct Sheet, **kosa, makosa**
Envelope, **bahasha**
Esprit de Corps, **heshima**
Europe, **Ulaya**
European, **Mzungu**
Even numbers, (mily) **watu wa tu tu**
Evening, **jioni**
Every, **kila**
Expen es, **garama**
Expensive, **gali**
Explode, to, **ku-pasuka**
Explosives, **baruti**
Extinguish a light, to, **ku-zima**
Eyes, **macho**

F

Face, **uso**
Fail, to, **ku-kosa**
Fall, to, **ku-anguka**
Falsehood, **uwongo**
Far, **mbali**
as Far as, **mpaka**
Farm, **shamba**
Fast, **upesi**
Fasten, to, **ku-funga**
Fat, **mafuta**, (*noun*) **nene** (*adj.*)
Fat, to become, **ku-nona**
Father, **baba**
Fault, **makosa**
Fear, to, **ku-ogopa**
Feed, to, **ku-lisha**

Female, **muke ;** *pl.* **wake**
Fence, a, **boma**
Fever, **homa**
Few, **chache**
Field, **shamba**
Field glasses, **darubini**
Fierce, **kali**
Fifty, **hamsini**
Fig tree, **makuyu**
Fight, to, **ku-pigana**
File, **tupa**
Fill, to, **ku-jaza**
Find, to, **ku-ona**
Fine, **mzuri**
Finger, **kidole**
Finish, to, **ku-maliza**
Finished, to be, **kwisha**
Fire, **moto**
Fire a gun, to, **ku-piga bunduki**
Firewood, **kuni**
Firm, **imara**
First, **ya kwanza**
Fish, **samaki**
Fist, **konde, ngumi**
Fitting, to be, **ku-faa**
Five, **tano**
Flag, **bandera**
Flay, to, **ku-chuna**
Flea, **kiroboto**
Flesh, **nyama**
Flog, to, **ku-piga**
Flour, **unga**
Flowers, **maua**
Fly, a, **inzi,** *pl.* **mainzi**
Fly, to, **ku-ruka**
Fold, to, **ku-kunja**
Follow, to, **ku-fuata**
Food, **chakula**
Fool, a, **mjinga**
Foot, **miguu**
Footstep, **hatua**
For, **kwa**
Forbid, to, **ku-kataza**
Force, **nguvu**
Ford, a, **kivuko**
Foreigner, **mgeni**
Forest, in the, **musitoni**
Forget, to, **ku-sahau**
Forgive, to, **ku-samehe**
Fork, **uma**

Formerly, **zamani**
Fortune, **bahati**
Forty, **arobaini**
Forward, **mbele**
Four, **ine**
Fowl, **kuku**
Fresh, **mbichi**
Friday, **Jumaa**
Friend, **rafiki**
Frog, **chura**
From, **kwa**
in Front of, **mbele ya**
Fruit, **matunda**
Fry, to, **ku-karanga, ku-pika frai**
Full, to be, **ku-jaa**
Full, to be, with eating, **ku-shiba**

G

Gain, **faida**
Game, a, **mchezo**
Garden, vegetable, **shamba**
Garden, flower, **bustani**
Gate, **mlango**
Gather, to, **ku-kusanya**
Get, to, **ku-pata**
Get down from, to, **ku-shuka**
Ghee, **samli**
Gift, **bakshishi**
Giraffe, **twiga**
Girl, **ndito**
Give back, to, **ku-rudisha**
Give, to, **kupa, ku-toa**
Glad, to be, **ku-furai**
Glass, **bilauri**
Go, to, **kwenda**
Go away, to, **ku-toka, ku-ondoka**
Go back, to, **ku-rudi**
Go bad, rot. to, **ku-oza**
Go downhill, to, **ku-teremuka**
Go out, to, **ku-toka**
Goat, **mbuzi**
God, **Mungu**
Gold, **thahabu**
Gold dust, **pesa**
Gonorrhea, **kisonono**
Good, **mzuri, vyema!**
Goods, **mali**
Gourd, **kibuyu**
Government, **serikali**
Government station, **boma**

Gramophone, kinanda
Grass, nyasi, majani
Gratis, bure
Grease, mafuta
Great, mkubwa, kuu
Green, rangi ya majani
Greet, to, ku-salimu
Grenade. bombom
Grind, to, ku-saga
Groom. a, sais
Ground, inchi
Ground-nuts, njugu
Guard, a, mlinzi
Guard, to, ku-chunga
Guard, to (Mil.), ku-linda
Guardroom, kwota gaad
Guide, kiongozi
Guinea-fowl, kanga
Gun, bunduki
Gunpowder, baruti
Gutter, fereji

H

Hair, nywele
Half, nusu
Halt, to, ku-simama
Hammer, nyundo
Hand, mkono
Handle, kipini
Happiness, heri
Happy, to be, ku-furai
Hard, ngumu
Hare, sangura
Harlot, malaya
Harm, to, ku-thuru
Harvest, mavuno
Hartebeeste, kongoni
Hat, kofia
Hatchet, shoka
Hate, to, ku-chukia
Have, to, kuwa na
Haversack, mkoba
Having, mwenyi
He, yeye, huyu
Head, kichwa
Healthy, mzima
Hear, to, ku-sikia
Heart, moyo
Heat, moto
Heaven, mbingu

Heavy, mzito
Heel, kisigino
Heifer, mtamba
Height, urefu
Help, to, ku-saidia
Help, msaada
Her, yake
Herdsman, mchungi
Here, hapa
Hide, to, ku-ficha
High, mrefu
Hill, kilima
Hinder, to, ku-zuia
Hinges, pata
Hippopotamus, kiboko
His, yake
Hit, to ku-piga
Hoe, jembe
Hold, to, ku-shika, ku-kamata
Hole, shimo, tundu
Homestead, mtaa
Honest, wa haki
Honey, asali
Honour, heshima
Horn, pembe
Horizon, Upeo wa macho
Horse, farasi
Hot, ya moto
Hour, saa
House, nyumba
How ? Namna gani ?
How many ? ngapi ?
Hump, a, nundu
Hundred, mia
Hunger, njaa
Hunt, to, ku-winda
Hurt, to. ku-umiza, ku-uma
Husband, mume, bwana
Hut, nyumba, kibanda
Hyaena, fisi, nyangau

I

I, mimi
Idiot, pumbavu
Idle, mvivu
If, kama
Ill, mgonjwa
Immediately, mara-moja, sasa-hivi
In, ndani, katika
In vain, bure

Increase, to, **ku-ongeza**
Indian, **Muhindi**
Indian corn, **mahindi**
Indiarubber **mpira**
Inform, to, **ku-ambia, ku-harifu**
Ink, **wino**
Injure, to, **ku-thuru**
Inoculate, to, **ku-chanja**
Insect, **dudu**
Inside, **ndani**
Instead of, **mahali pa**
Intelligence, **akili**
Into, **katika**
Iron, **chuma**
Iron for clothes, **pasi**
Island, **kisiwa**
Its, **yake**

J

Jersey, **fulana**
Journey, **safari**
Judge, to, **ku-hukumu**
Judgment, **hukumu**
Jump, to, **ku-ruka**
Just, only, **tu**

K

Kettle, **birika**
Key, **ufunguo**
Kick, to, **ku-piga teke**
Kidney, **figo**
Kill to **ku-ua,**
Kill for food, to, **ku-chinja**
Kind (sort), **namna**
Kitchen, **jikoni**
Knee, **goti**
Knife, **kisu**
Knock, to, at door, **ku-piga hodi**
Know, to, **ku-jua**

L

Labour, **kazi**
Lack, to, **ku-angaika**
Ladder, **ngazi**
Lamp, **taa**
Land, **inchi**
Large, **mkubwa**
Last, **ya mwisho, wa jana**
Late, to be, **ku-chelewa**
Later, **halafu**
Latrine, **choo.**
Laugh, to, **ku-cheka**

Lay eggs, to, **ku-zaa mayai**
Lazy, **mvivu**
Lead, **risasi**
Leaf, **jani,** *pl.* **majani**
Lean on, to, ku-tegemea
Learn, to, **ku-jifunza**
Leather, **ngozi**
Leave, **ruhusa, ruksa**
Leave, to, **ku-wacha**
Left hand, **mkono wa kushoto**
Leg, **mguu**
Leisure, **nafasi**
Lemons, **ndimu, malimau**
Lend, to, **ku-kopesha**
Length, **urefu**
Leopard, **chui**
Less, by, **kasu**
Lessen, to, **ku-punguza**
Let, to, **ku-wacha**
Letter, **barua**
Letter, of alphabet, **harufu**
Lid, **kifuniko**
Lie, a, **urongo**
Lie down, to, **ku-lala**
Lift up, to, **ku-inua**
Like, to be, **ku-fanana**
Like, to, **ku-penda**
Lime (chalk), **chokaa**
Lime juice, **ndimu**
Line, **mstari**
Lion, **simba**
Lips, **midomo**
Listen, to, **ku-sikiliza**
Little, **kidogo, mdogo**
Live at, to, **ku-kaa**
Liver, **ini**
Load, **mzigo**
Loaf, **mkate**
Lock, a, **kufuli**
Locust, **nzige**
Long, **mrefu**
Look, to, **ku-angalia, ku-tezama**
Look after, to, **ku-chunga**
Look for, to, **ku-tafuta**
Looking-glass, **kioo**
Loose, to be, **ku-legea**
Lose, to, **ku-poteza**
Loss, **hasara**
Lost, to become, **ku-potea**
Love, to, **ku-penda**
Luck, **bahati**

M

Machine, **mtambo**
Machine gun, **bombom, takataka**
Maize, **mahindi**
Maize meal, **posho**
Make, to, **ku-fanya**
Male animal, **ndume**
Male person, **mwana-mume**
Man, **mutu**
Mango, **mwembe**
Many, **nyingi, mingi**
Mark, **alama**
Market, **soko, sokoni**
Marriage, **arusi**
Marry, to a wife, **ku-oa**
Married, to be, to a husband,
  ku-olewa
Marsh, **ziwa**
Masai homestead, **manyata**
Masculine, **mume**
Mast, **mlingoti**
Master, **bwana**
Mat, **mkeka**
Matches, **kibiriti**
Matter, to, **ku-thuru**
Mattress, **godoro**
Me, **mimi**
Meaning, **maana**
Measure, to, **ku-pima**
Meat, **nyama**
Medicine, **dawa**
Meet, to, **ku-kutana**
Men, **watu**
Mend, to, **ku-tengeneza**
Middle, **kati-kati**
Milk, **maziwa**
Milk, to, **ku-kama**
Millet, **mtama, wimbi**
Mine, **yangu**
Minute, a, **dakika**
Mirror, **kioo**
Miss, to, **ku-kosa**
Mistake, **kosa**, *pl.* **makosa**
Mix, to, **ku-changanya**
Mohammedan, **Mwislamu**
Monday, **juma tatu**
Money, **fedha, rupia, shilingi**
Monkey, **kima, nyanya**
Month, **mwezi**
Moon, **mwezi**
More, **zaidi, ingine**

Morning, **asubuhi**
Mosquito, **mbu, umbu**
Mother, **mama**
Mountain, **mlima, kilima**
Mouse, **panya**
Move house, to, **ku-hama**
Much, **tele, sana, mingi**
Mud, **tope, matope**
Mufti, **nguo za raiya**
Mule, **nyumbu**
Mushrooms, **vioga**
My, **yangu**

N

Nail, iron, **msumari**
Nail, human, **ukucha**
Naked, **tupu**
Name, **jina**
Narrow, **nyembamba**
Near, **karibu**
Necessary, it is, **lazma**
Neck, **shingo**
Needle, **sindano**
New, **mpya**
News, **habari**
Newspaper, **gazeti**
Next (year), **(mwaka) ujao**
Night, **usiku**
Nine, **tisa**
Ninety, **tisini**
No, **hapana, siyo**
Noise, **kelele**
Nonsense, **upuzi**
North, **kaskazini**
Nose, **pua**
Not, **hapana, si**
Not yet, **bado**
Note, **barua**
Nothing, **hapana kitu**
Now, **sasa**
Number, **hesabu**

O

Oath, **kiapo**
Obey, to, **ku-tii, ku-fuata amri**
Odd numbers (military), **watu wa**
  wan wan
Of, **ya, wa**
Often, **mara nyingi**
Oil, **mafuta**
Old man, **mzee**
Olive tree, **matamayo**
On, **juu ya**

F

Once, **mara moja**
One, **moja**
Onions, **vitunguu**
Only, **tu**
Open, **wazi**
Open, to, **ku-fungua**
Open bush country, **vishakani**
Opportunity, **nafasi**
Opposite bank, the, **ngambo**
Or, **au**
Orange, **chungwa**; *pl.* **machun-gwa**
Order, **amri**
Order, to, **ku-amuru**
Ostrich, **mbuni**
Other, **ingine**
Our, **yetu**
Outside, **inje**
Over, **juu ya**
Overcome, to, **ku-shinda**
Overturn, to, **ku-pindua**
Owner, **mwenyewe**
Ox, **ngombe**

P

Pace, a, **hatua**
Padlock, **kufuli**
Pain, to, **ku-uma**
Paint, **rangi**
Pair, **jozi**
Paper, **karatasi**
Pass, to, **ku-pita**
Path, **njia**
Pawpaw, **papayi**
Pay, to, **ku-lipa**
Peas, **binzi**
Peg, a, **kigingi**
Pen, Pencil, **kalamu**
People, **watu**
Pepper, **pilipili**
Perhaps, **labda**
Person, **mtu**
Perspiration, **jasho**
Photograph a, **piksha**
Piano, **kinanda**
Pick-axe, **sururu**
Pick up, to, **ku-lokota**
Piece, **kipande**
Pierce, to, **ku-toboa**
Pig, **nguruwe**
Pillar, **nguzo**

Pillow, **mto**
Pineapples, **mananasi**
Pipe, tobacco, **kiko**
     ,,   water, **fereji**
Pit, a, **shimo**
Place, **mahali**
Place, to, **ku-weka**
Plague, the, **tauni**
Plane, carpenter's, **randa**
Plant, to, **ku-panda**
Plate, **sahani**
Play, to, **ku-cheza**
Plenty, **tele**
Plough, a, **jembe**
Plough, to, **ku-lima**
Pocket a, **kifuko**
Point, a, **ncha**
Poison, **sumu**
Pole, a, **miti, boriti, mlingote**
Policeman, **askari**
Poor man a, **maskini**
Porcupine, **nungu**
Porter, **mpagazi**
Possessions, **mali**
Post, a wooden, **nguzo, miti**
Potatoes, **viazi**
Pound, a, **ratili**
Pour out, to, **ku-mwaga**
Pregnancy, **mimba**
Prepare to,   **ku-tengeneza, ku-weka tayari**
Present, a, **bakshishi, zawadi**
Pretty, **mzuri**
Prevent, to, **ku-zuia**
Price, **bei**
Print, to, **ku-piga chapa**
Prison, **gereza**
Prisoner (military), **mabusu**
Profit, **faida**
Property, **mali**
Pull, to, **ku-vuta**
Pull up, to, **ku-ngoa**
Punishment, **athabu**
Push, to, **ku-sukuma**
Put, to, **ku-tia, ku-weka**
Put right, to, **ku-tengeneza**

Q

Quarrel, to, **ku-gombana**
Quarter, a, **robo**

Question, **maulizo, maswale**
Question, to, **ku-uliza**
Quickly, **upesi**
Quite, **kabisa**

R

Rag, **kitambaa**
Railway train, **gari la moshi**
Rain, **mvua**
Raise, to, **ku-inua**
Ram home, to, **ku-shindilia**
Range, a rifle, **shabaha**
Rat, **panya**
Rations, **posho**
Raw, **mbichi**
Razor, **wembe**
Reach, to, **ku-fika**
Read, to, **ku-soma**
Ready, **tayari**
Reap, to, **ku-vuna**
Reason, **sababu**
Red, **nyekundu**
Refuse, to, **ku-kataa**
Regulations, **kanuni**
Reinforcements, **msaada**
Rejoice, to, **ku-furai**
Remain, to, **ku-kaa**
Remain over, to, **ku-baki**
Remember, to, **ku-kumbuka**
Remind, to, **ku-kumbusha**
Resemble, to, **ku-fanana na**
Rest, to, **ku-pumzika**
Return, to, **ku-rudi**
Reward, **bakshishi**
Rhinoceros, **kifaru**
Ribs, **mbavu**
Rice, **mchele**
Rice, cooked, **wali**
Rice, unpolished, **mpunga**
Riches, **mali**
Ride, to, **ku-panda**
Rifle, **bunduki**
Right hand, **mkono wa kulia**
Rind, **ganda ;** *pl.* **maganda**
Ripen, to, **ku-iva**
River, **mtoni**
River bed, dry, **mkondo**
Road, **bara-bara, njia**
Roast, **ku-pika rost**

Rocks, **mwamba, maawe**
Roll call, **tamaam**
Roof, a, **dari**
Room, a, **chumba**
Roots, **mizizi**
Rope, **kamba**
Rot, to, **ku-oza**
Rotten, **mbovu**
Rub, to, **ku-sugua**
Run away, to, **ku-toroka**
Run, to, **ku-kimbia**
Rust, **kutu**

S

Sack, **gunia**
Saddle, **matandiko**
Saliva, **mate**
Salt, **chumvi**
Sand, **mchanga**
Saturday, **Juma mosi**
Saucer, **kisahani**
Savage, **kali**
Savoury, a, **tosti**
Saw, **msumeno**
Say, to, **ku-sema**
Scabbard, **ala**
Scales, weighing, **mizani**
Scissors, **makasi**
Scout, to, **ku-peleleza**
Sea, **bahari**
Search, to, **ku-tafuta**
Seat, **kiti**
Secretary, **karani**
See, to, **ku-ona**
Seed, **mbegu**
Seek, to, **ku-tafuta**
Seize, to, **ku-kamata**
Self, **mwenyewe**
Sell, to, **ku-uza**
Send, to, **ku-peleka**
Send back, to, **ku-rudisha**
Sense, **akili**
Sentence (judgment), **hukumu**
Sergeant **sajenti, shawesh**
Seven, **saba**
Seventeen, **kumi na saba**
Seventy, **sabaini**
Sew, to, **ku-shona**
Shadow, **kivuli**
Sharp, **kali**
Shave, to, **ku-nyoa**

She, yeye
Shed, kibanda
Sheep, kondoro
Shell, a (mily.), risasi
Shell (bursting), baruti
Shield, ngao
Ship, meli
Shiver, to, ku-tetemeka
Shoes, viatu
Shoot, to, ku-piga bunduki
Shop, duka
Short, mfupi
Shoulders, mabega
Shout, to, ku-lia
Show, to, ku-onyesha
Shut, to, ku-funga
Sick, mgonjwa
Sick, to be, ku-tapika
Sickness, ugonjwa
Side, upande
Side, at the, kando-kando
Sieve, a, kichungo
Sieve, to, ku-chunga
Silent, to be, ku-nyamaza
Silver, fetha
Sim-sim oil, mafuta ya uto
Since, tangu
Sing, to, ku-imba
Sink, to, ku-zama
Sir, bwana
Sisal, makonge,
Sister, ndugu mwana-muke
Sit, to, ku-keti
Sitting-room, sebuleni
Six, sita
Sixteen, kumi na sita
Sixty, sitini
Skin, ngozi
Sleep, usingizi
Sleep, to, ku-lala
Slowly, polepole
Small, kidogo, mdogo
Small-pox, ndui
Smart, maridadi
Smell, harufu
Smell, to, ku-nuka
Smoke, moshi
Snake, nyoka
Snuff, tumbaku
Soap, sabuni
Soldier, asikari
Son, mwana

Soon, karibu
Sore, kidonda
Sort, namna
South, kusini
Sow, to, ku-panda
Space, nafasi
Spade, a, mwiko
Spear, mkuke
Spectacles, miwani
Spill, to, ku-mwaga
Spirit, roho
Split, to, ku-pasua
Spoil, to, ku-haribu
Spoilt, to be, ku-haribika
Spoon, kijiko
Squeeze, to, ku-kamua
Stand, to, ku-simama
Star, a, nyota
Stay, to, ku-kaa
Steal, to, ku-iba
Steamship, meli
Step, hatua
Stick, fito, fimbo, miti
Sting, to, ku-uma
Stir, to, ku-koroga
Stomach, tumbo
Stones, mawe
Stop, to, ku-simama
Straight, sawa-sawa
Straighten, to, ku-nyosha,
Strange, mgeni   [nyorosa
Stranger, mgeni
Strength, nguvu
Stretcher, a, machera
Strike, to, ku-piga
Stripe, a (N.C.O.), tepe
String, uzi
Suffice, to, ku-tosha
Sugar, sukari
Suit, to, ku-faa
Sulphur, kibiriti
Sun, jua
Sunday, Juma pili
Sweat, jasho
Sweep, to, ku-fagia
Sweet, tamu
Swell, to, ku-fura, ku-vimba
Swim, to, ku-ogelea
Sword, panga
Syphilis, tego
Syrup, asali

T

Table, **meza**
Tail, **mkia**
Take away, to, **ku-ondoa**
Take off, to, **ku-toa**
Tall, **mrefu**
Tarpaulin, **shandarua**, tandarua
Tax, **kodi**
Tea, **chai**
Teach, to, **ku-fundisha**
Teacher, **mwalimu**
Teeth, **meno**
Telegraph, **simu**
Telephone, **simu**
Telescope, **darubini**
Tell, to, **ku-ambia**
Ten, **kumi**
Tent, **hema**
Tent-pegs, **vigingi**
Than, **kuliko**
Thanks, **asante**
That (demonst.), **ile**
  „ (conjunction), **kwamba**
Their, **yao**
Then, **halafu**
There, **huko**
These, **hii, hizi**
They, **wao, hawa**
Thick, **nene**
Thief, **mwivi**
Thin, **nyembamba**
Thin, to get, **ku-konda**
Thine, **yako**
Thing, **kitu**
Think, to, **ku-thani**
Thirst, **kiu**
Thirteen, **kumi na tatu**
Thirty, **thelathini**
This, **hii**
Thorn, **mwiba**
Those, **ile**
Thousand, **elfu**
Thread, **uzi**
Three, **tatu**
Throw, to, **ku-tupa**
Thunder, **ngurumo**, radi
Thursday, **alhamisi**
Thus, **vile, vile vile**
Thy, **yako**
Tie, to, **ku-funga**
Tighten, to, **ku-kaza**

Time, **saa, wakati**
Time, a, **mara**
Tin, **mkebe**
Tired, to be, **ku-choka**
Tobacco, **tumbaku**
To-day, **leo**
Toe, **kidole**
Together, **pamoja**
Tomato, **nyanya**
To-morrow, **kesho**
Tongue, **ulimi**
Tool, a, **chuma**
Tough, **gumu**
Town, **mji**
Trap, **mtego**
Tread on, to, **ku-kanyaga**
Tree, **miti**
Tremble, to, **ku-tetemeka**
Trench, **handaki**
Tribe, **kabila**
Trouble, **matata**
Trousers, **suruale**
Truth, **kweli**
Try, to, **ku-jaribu**
Tuesday, **juma ine**
Tumbler, **bilauri, gilasi**
Turkey, a, **bata mzinga, nguru-guru**
Turn, to, **ku-pindua**
Tusk, **pembe**
Twenty, **ishirini**
Twist, to, **ku-sokota**
Two, **mbili, wawili**
Tyre, **mpira**

U

Ulcer, **kidonda**
Umbrella, **mwavuli**
Uncivilised, **shenzi**
Under, **chini ya**
Understand, to, **ku-fahemu**
Unfasten, to, **ku-fungua**
Unripe, **mbichi**
Until, **hata, mpaka**
Up, **juu**
Upon, **juu ya**
Upset, to, **ku-pindua**
Urinate, to, **ku-kojoa**
Urine, **mikojo**
Us, **sisi**
Use, to, **ku-tumia**
Useless, **bure**

V

Valley, **bonde**
Value, **thamani**
Vegetables, **mboga**
Verandah, **baraza**
Very, **sana**
Village, **mji, kijiji**
Vine, **mzabibu**
Vinegar, **siki**
Visible, to be, **ku-onekana**
Voice, **sauti**
Vomit, **ku-tapika**

W

Wages, **mshahara**
Waggon, **gari**
Wait, to, **ku-ngoja**
Wake up, to, **ku-amuka**
Wake, to cause to, **ku-amusha**
Walk, to, **ku-tembea**
Walking-stick, **fimbo**
Wall, **ukuta**
Want, to, **ku-taka**
War, **vita**
Wash oneself, to, **ku-nawa**
Wash clothes, to, **ku-fua**
Washerman, **dobi**
Waste, to, **ku-poteza**
Watch, **saa**
Water, **maji**
Water-buck, **nkulu**
Water-jar, **mtungi**
Way, **njia**
We, **sisi**
Wealth, **mali**
Weapon, **silaha**
Wear, to, **ku-vaa**
Weary, to be, **ku-choka**
Wed, to, **ku-oa**
Wedding, **arusi**
Wednesday, **juma tano**
Week, **wiki**
Weep, to, **ku-lia**
Weigh, to, **ku-pima**
Well, a, **kisima**
Well, (Adverb) **mzuri**
West, **magaribi**
Wet, **maji-maji**
What? **nini?**
Wheat, **ngano**

Wheel, **gurudumo, mguu**
When, as, **kama**
When? **saa ngapi? siku gani?**
Where? **wapi?**
Whether, **kwamba**
Which? **gani?**
While, **wakati**
Whip, **msharidi**
Whistle, **mbinda, firimbi**
White, **nyeupe, mweupe**
Who? **nani ?**
Whole, **mzima**
Whore, **malaya**
Why? **kwa nini ?**
Wick, **utambi**
Wide, **pana**
Wife, **bibi**
Wind, **upepo, baridi**
Window, **dirisha**
Wipe, to, **ku-futa, ku-pangusa**
Wire, **sengenge**
Wireless, **simu ya upepo**
Witchcraft, **uchawi**
Witch-doctor (bad), **Mchawi**
Witch-doctor (good), **mganga**
With, **na, pamoja na**
Withhold, to, **ku-nyima**
Witness, **shahidi**
Woman, **mwanamuke**
Women, **wana-wake**
Wood, **miti**
Words, **maneno**
Work, **kazi**
Worry, to, **ku-sumbua**
Wound, **jeraha**
Write to, **ku-andika**

Y

Year, **mwaka**
Yes, **ndiyo**
Yesterday, **jana**
Yonder, **kule**
You (*sing.*), **wewe**, *pl.* **ninyi**
Young, **kijana**
Your (*sing.*), **yako**, *pl.* **yenu**

Z

Zebra, **punda milia**

KEY TO EXERCISES.

PRONUNCIATION. P. 7.

These two cars are very cheap. Who may you be please ? How nice you are looking to-day, so bright, so gay. The stage coach came quite soon. Snakes are hard to see. The pool seems deep. Peter gave me my tea too late. A snowy day makes me cold, a stove to heat the room would be good.

GREETINGS. P. 8.

Jambo Bwana. Jambo Memsaab. Jambo Murunga. Habari gani hapa. Habari mzuri tu, Bwana. Ndio, Memsaab. Hapana, Bwana. Kwa heri Bwana. Kwa heri Memsaab. Sumile kwa Bwana.

N- CLASS NOUNS WITH ADJECTIVES. P. 11.

Pembe kali. Nyama ngumu. Nyama kali. Ndizi mbichi. Kengele kidogo. Damu nyekundu. Ndoo nyeupe. Siagi mzuri. Ndugu ingine. Siafu mingi. Ngambo. Merikani mbaya. Kofia mzuri. Saa mpya. Ngombe nyeusi. Risasi mzito. Nguo Nyeusi. Rungu ingine. Nazi nyingi. Kahawa mzuri. Rangi nyekundu. Pamba nyeupe. Pembe mkubwa. Ndugu muke. Dasturi ingine. Ngoma mzuri. Siku kuu. Siku kuu. Deni mkubwa. Ngoma mzito. Baruti nyeusi. Tupa kali. Nyama mbovu. Nguvu mpya. Rafiki mume. Baba kali. Samaki nyembamba. Mbuzi kali. Inchi mzuri. Njugu mingi. Bunduki mzito. Nusu ingine. Nyundo mzima. Ndama mpya. Nyuki nyingi. Asali nyeusi. Nyumba mkubwa. Saa ngapi.

P. 12.

Ndugu na njaa sana. Safari mrefu na hasara mingi. Ngazi namna gani. Taa gani. Ngozi ngumu. Barua ngapi. Ndimu chungu sana. Nzige mingi sana na ndege mingi. Ngombe ndume. Dawa chungu sana. Mama mzuri. Nyumbu kali. Sindano kali. Habari mzuri. Hesabu mkubwa (or mingi sana). Ngombe mvivu. Karatasi nene na karatasi nyembamba. Njia nyembamba mrefu. Kalamu nyeusi ngumu. Nguzo mrefu. Sahani kidogo mzuri. Sumu kali. Nungu na sindano mingi sana. Faida gani ? Mali kidogo. Nafasi kidogo. Nafasi wazi. Bara-bara mrefu sana. Kamba mzima. Kondoro na njaa. Ngao ngumu. Ngozi tupu. Nyoka mzima. Sabuni gani ? Nafasi kidogo sana. Meza nyeupe kidogo. Hema tupu. Kiu sana. Nyanya mbichi. Fereji wazi. Mboga mbovu. Vinega chungu. Fimbo nyeupe mfupi. Nganu mbichi. Dawa kali sana. Kazi ngumu mingi sana. Namna gani ?

DEMONSTRATIVES AND NUMERALS. P. 13.

Siafu ine ile. Kofia mkubwa mbili. Saa ngapi ? Saa tatu. Rungu mzito mkubwa tano hii. Namna hii. Namna hii. Nyumba tupu sita ile. Ngazi mrefu tano hii. Taa moja. Risasi kumi. Barua arobaini. Kalamu nane. Sindano kali saba. Sahani tisa ile Saa.

moja na nusu. Hema kumi na mbili. Barua kumi na sita na kalamu tisa. Meza tisini na tatu. Fimbo mia mbili, sabaini na ine. Siku mia tano, thamanini na moja na robo. Ndizi ishirini na tano. Bunduki mfupi sita na risasi mzito sana thelathini na saba. Nguzo nyeusi mrefu hamsini na ine. Kofia mia tano, sitini na moja. Nyanya mbovu elfu kumi na mbili, mia sita, thamanini na saba na ndizi mbichi elfu thelathini na ine, mia saba, ishirini na moja.

Karatasi nyeupe hii mzito. Dawa ile chungu. Nganu ile mbichi. Ndoo kumi hii nyeupe. Ngozi hii gumu sana. Chai hii kali sana. Kazi hii mbaya sana. Kamba mkubwa sana hii mzito sana. Nyoka mingi sana siku hizi.

M- CLASS (ANIMATE). P. 14.

Mutu huyu. Wazee wavivu watatu. Wazungu warefu watano. Wana waume wawili na mwana muke moja. Mutu mzee sana. Mutu mjinga sana. Wageni hawa. Hawa wageni. Wazee wake wadogo hawa weusi sana. Mutu huyu mrefu hawa wafupi. Nyumba ya mzungu. Mtoto wa mzungu. Dawa ya mgonjwa. Wachungi hawa wajinga. Nguo ya washenzi hawa nyeusi. Washenzi weusi.

M- CLASS. P. 15 & 16.

Milima hii mrefu. Mikono mbili. Mikono moja. Mwanzo mbaya. Mwili mzima. Mifupa ngumu. Mizigo hii mzito sana. Mitumbwi mkubwa mbili. Mpishi hii mvivu sana. Mwenzi wa mwalimu mulevi. Mizabibu mingi. Milango nene hii. Mguu ya mutu huyu. Mchezo ya mtoto. Hii mikuke ya mchungi, mpishi mwenyewe ya mkuke hii. Shauri ya mungu. Moyo ya ngombe. Midomo nyekundu mbili. Mkate ya mpishi mbaya sana. Mlingoti mrefu hii. Milima mrefu ile. Mwezi nyekundu. Muto nyeupe ine. Mpaka hii mtoni. Mguu ya mgonjwa. Bwana mrefu. Dawa ya muchawi. Mwiko ya mutu mweusi. Mkia ya nyama. Hii mitego ya mzungu. Mwezi ya siku thelathini. Memsaab mbili. Ngambo mtoni. Mwanzo ya miti. Hii mitungi ingine. Mwisho ya mwaka. Watu wa miti. Moshi ya moto nyeusi sana. Mwivi ya ngombe. Mwili ya mtoto mwana muke. Mwiba nyembamba. Mlingote ya nguvu. Mikebe tupu ishirini. Msharidi ya nguvu.

INTERROGATIVES. P. 17

Nani wewe ? Wapi watu ? Hawa ngapi ? Nani mzee huyu ? Sisi wageni. Mimi mzungu. Hawa weusi (or watu weusi). Nini hii ? Miti gani hii ? Miti gani ? Mimi mwenyewe mgonjwa. Hawa wachawi. Huyu mwalimu. Nani mtoto ? Mtoto wa nani ? Wapi nyumba ya mwenyewe ya ngombe hii ? Huyu mzee. Huyu mgonjwa. Mgonjwa gani ? Mgonjwa ya mguu. Mguu gani ? Wewe mjinga.

VERB, KU-, ME-, TA-. P. 18.

Nimepiga kengele. Utapiga bunduki. Atapiga pampa. Tutapiga hema wapi ? Amepiga pasi. Watapiga kelele sana. Umepiga hodi ? Mvua itapiga. Nimepiga randa kwa milango. Watapiga simu. Umepiga iani wapi ? Atapiga firimbi.

VERB. OTHER TENSES. P. 19.

Tulipiga milango na nyundo. Piga sana ! Twapiga pasi. Ulipiga nani ? Alipiga mimi. Napiga kengele. Walipiga ngoma. Twapiga ngoma. Nalipiga bunduki. Piga kengele ! Wanapiga ngombe. Alipiga mtoto. Nalipiga hodi. Twapiga kelele sana. Piga pasi nguo hii. Ilipiga nyumba. Ulipiga pasi nguo hii mbaya sana. Lete sahani mbili. Mwalimu alipiga randa kwa milango. Mzee na mimi tulipiga kelele sana. Mchungi na mtoto wamepiga ngombe. Mvua itapiga ? Mtoto anapiga mbuzi. Nyundo ilipiga baruti. Mvua inapiga sana. Mpishi anapiga muchawi. Wamepiga nyama na bunduki. Napiga mulevi na miti. Mzee huyu na mimi tumepiga njugu na rungu.

VERBS. FIRST VOCABULARY. P. 20.

Naweza pika. Twakubali. Atasumbua mpishi. Nzige wameonekana. Mwalimu atafika. Omba taa. Nitaamuka. Alioga mtoni. Miti hii itazaa. Mwana muke amezaa. Mboga inachemuka. Dawa inachemuka. Alikopa kofia. Lete sahani sita. Nitajenga nyumba mpya. Nachoma karatasi hii. Nyumba inaungua. Umenunua ngombe ishirini. Angalia ! Chukua mizigo hii. Alikamata mkia ya ngombe. Huyu mwivi tu, alidanganya mpishi na sasa anadai mimi. Angalia kusafisha bunduki sana. Panda nguzo ile. Umerudi. Watoka wapi ? Nimefikiri shauri. Kazi inashinda mimi. Mpishi anapika. Mgonjwa anakohoa. Funika siagi. Wanalia sana. Umelima ndizi ?

OBJECTIVE PREFIXES. P. 21.

Nitamwuliza wapi mtoto. Mwambia huyu kuniita. Mwita ! Nyuki ameniuma. Nitawaona. Alikuona. Nipa pembe ya ngombe. Mupa. Nitawapa dawa. Amemwua. Namjua. Watanijua. Mguu hii inaniuma sana. Mutu huyu atamwonyesha mpishi kupika mkate. Utamwambia ? Hapana, nitamwambia mwenyewe. Wameniambia.

TABLE OF PREFIXES. P. 21.

Ninakupiga. Mwatupiga. Watawapiga. Amempiga. Tuliwapiga. Wanipiga. Tunawapiga. Imenipiga. Itakupiga. Umetupiga. Wanatupiga. Nalikupiga. Tutampiga. Alimpiga. Anampiga. Inanipiga. Walikupiga. Nimewapiga. Utatupiga.

VERBS. SECOND VOCABULARY. P. 23.

Mgonjwa amepona. Alichelewa kuingia nyumba. Tutateremuka milima. Chimba fereji. Wafanya nini ? Miti mingi imeanguka, buruta na ngombe. Anika nguo hii. Imekwisha kauka. Umekosa. Wanona sana. Mimi naogopa nyoka, funga milango. Nalimpiga na alipigana na mimi. Nitamaliza mkate hii na nitashiba. Nalikwambia wewe kukunja nguo namna hii, umesahau ? Mpishi amelewa, mfukuza, nitapata ingine, umekwisha mwambia kutoka nyumba ? Nitatoa nganu ya nyumbu. Nitarudi. Siagi imeoza. Tangulia mimi. Ulisikia mimi kusaga nazi ? Tutamsaidia huyu kuficha taa ingine.

MONOSYLLABIC VERBS. P. 23.

Nitakuwa mgonjwa. Alikuwa mjinga. Utakwanza mwanzo, na utamaliza mwisho. Nitamaliza asali na asali itakwisha. Mgonjwa amekwisha kufa. Njoo ! tutakwanza kazi. Walikula mkate. Bwana siagi imekwisha, mtoto amekula. Mimi nitakwenda nyumba, wewe utakuja ? Kwenda ! Toka ! Njooni

POSSESSIVE PRONOUNS. P. 25 & 26.

Au mzee, au mwenzi yake, au wote wawili, wamezuia mpishi kugombana na mtoto. Mtoto anashika kamba ya ngombe, twamwita Mshika-kamba. Naweza kuongeza hesabu ya ngombe yetu kama wewe utasaidia mimi. Mbuzi yako yote wameruka mtoni, wasikia? Lete bunduki yangu, mimi natoka kuchinja nyama. Wewe wachelewa tena, labda wewe mgonjwa? Sasa wafanyaje? Wacha tu! Inua taa, natafuta sabuni. Kama wasikiliza sana labda utasikia nyama. Watazama nini? Angalia sana mifupa hii, nipa ingine namna hii kama waona. Kwenda, tafuta ngombe mpaka mtoni, halafu rudi ya kuniambia kama umeona. Mimi napenda ndizi sana. Legeza kamba hii tena mpaka mwisho yake. Umefanya kazi yako yote? Fanya nafasi ya sahani kumi na mbili. Mimi nitapima nganu hii kama wewe utapima ngazi hii. Nalikutana watu thelathini na mbili, lakini kama waliniona walificha, lakini naliwaita hawa halafu walikuja. Kama mimi nalipita watoto waliruka. Nitalipa watu wote halafu. Lazma kulokota tupa hii. Umeweka taa wapi? Labda ngombe nyeupe ile watavuta mzuri. Njooni ya kusukuma motokaa watu wote, sukuma sana, sukuma na nguvu! Tia sahani hapa sasa, halafu, kama nimekwisha kula, weka. Tandika nyumbu yangu! Umetandika meza? Nitaangalia taa na tengeneza, kisha nitatengeneza bunduki yangu. Mpishi anagombana sana na mtoto yake. Mjinga anakataa kusoma. Ni heri kuangalia kama wateremuka mlima sana.

PASSIVE VERBS. P. 27.

Mtoto alipigwa na mpishi. Kamba ya mizigo ya mzungu ilikatwa na mgeni na mwenzi yake. Mtungi yako imepinduka na mjinga huyu, na sasa imetoboka. Alioa halafu. Ataolewa tena. Asali yote imeharibika, mtoto alipindua ndoo na alimwaga asali. Nini? Ndio, ndoo ilipinduka na asali yote ilimwagika. Mzee ataitwa kama njugu imepimiwa. Mtoto alianguka na sahani yote ilivunjika. Mtoto huyu mbaya sana, amevunja sahani tena. Mlango imefungwa. Mwana muke atazaa saa ngapi? Bwana, mtoto amekwisha zaliwa. Jembe imeharibika, mguu yake imevunjika, na imepinduka. Lazma kuchoma ngozi ya nyanya hii, na karatasi ile imechomiwa?

CAUSATIVE VERBS. P. 28.

Kama waamusha huyu mara ingine ataamuka mara moja. Kwenda kuchemusha maji. Lakini Bwana, maji imekwisha chemuka. Rudi hapa. Rudisha saa yangu. Lakini kama nakopesha wewe sasa, wewe utakopa tena. Washa moto na kuja ya kuniambia kama inawaka mzuri. Ndoo hii inajaa, mwaga na jaza mara ingine. Lakini Bwana mimi mgonjwa sana, mwili yangu yote inaniuma. Lazma mimi kutia dawa kwa mguu yako, lakini nitaumiza wewe. Kama nacheza na huyu atacheka mara nyingi. Napenda siagi, asali inapendeza mimi tena. Wewe umepoteza barua yangu? Hapana Bwana, hapana mimi, lakini imepotea tu. Kama wakumbusha mimi mara mbili nitakumbuka. Kama waonyesha huyu ataona na atajua siku ingine. Simama hapa mwenyewe, na simamisha miti hii. Sasa sikiliza, kwenda huko na simama, wasikia?

NEGATIVE VERBS. P. 30.

Usikataa. Hatutafurai. Kwa nini hukupumzika ? Hawapandi. Hatukusugua kutosha. Hutakimbia sana. Hawakukimbia wote. Hawa wamekimbia wote.

Mboga hapana kupaki, hata kidogo. Sikusema kufanya namna hii. Sitapeleka nguo, hapana kushonewa, bado. Kwa nini wewe hapana funga milango ? Nalikosa Bwana. Sitaki kwambia wewe kila siku. Nalisahau Bwana. Usisahau, siwezi kulala na milango wazi. Sitakaa hapa sababu nyama inanuka. Wewe hapana kufagia hapa kutosha. Hawezi kulala, na mguu yake imevimba sana. Mwambia kuketi na nitaangalia. Chukua ndoo hii na weka huko, halafu rudi hapa na toa ngozi ya nyanya hii. Ondoa ngozi na tupa. Nathani wewe wakosa, lakini nitafikiri na kwambia halafu, sipendi kukosa. Watafundisha watoto kutupa. Funga kamba hii na kaza sana. Mimi bado kuchoka, nitajaribu tena kufungua taa yangu na nguvu. Lakini haifai, wafanya na nguvu kidogo sana. Haithuru, sitaki kungoja, nitawacha sababu nataka tembea. Nimeomba mwenzi yangu kupeleka ngombe yangu kwa huyu, lakini anakataa, ananyima, na wanakonda kabisa. Nitaandika barua ingine. Lakini Bwana kazi hii ngumu sana, mimi nachoka kabisa.

SUBSTANTIVES KI-, VI-. P. 31 & 32.

Vilima virefu vitatu. Vijiko hivi vyote vyako. Kitu hiki hapana changu, na vile vitano vya mpishi. Weka vitu vile vyote katika chumba chake. Nataka kisahani kikubwa. Kula nyama mbichi kitu kibaya. Huyu Mswahili, anajua maneno yote ya kiswahili. Mzungu huyu anapenda dawa ya kizungu, lakini sisi weusi twapenda dawa ya kishenzi. Umeshona nguo yangu vizuri sana. Haifai kuchelewa hivi, na wewe mpishi, ulichelewa vili-vile. Kwenda kazi yako sasa hivi. Vyema ! Wafanya kazi yako vizuri siku hizi.

KI-, VI-, CLASS VOCABULARY. P. 33.

Hii vikapu yangu. Toa viatu ile ya kitanda. Sipendi kitabu hii hata kidogo. Safisha viatu yangu mara moja ! Mimi mgonjwa ya kifua. Lazma kufunga kila kifungo. Kiti hii hapana vunjika. Kwa nini kizibo imepotea ? Lete vikombe tatu. Kidole yako imevimba. Lete chakula sasa hivi. Kipini ya milango imetoka. Kichwa inaniuma sana. Kilima hii mrefu sana. Kiboko ameharibu kibanda yetu. Fungua kifuniko hii kwa kisu, halafu lete kibiriti. Chuma ilianguka na ilivunja kioo hii kwa kipande mingi. Sipendi vitunguu, lakini napenda viazi na vioga. Nipa kitambaa ya mkono ingine na chukua kitambaa hii kwa memsaab, katika chumba ya chakula. Boy ! Nimepoteza kiko yangu. Mimi naona bwana, katika kinanda. Kama wasikiliza sana utaweza kusikia kifaru kufanya kelele. Safisha viatu hii tena na rangi nyeusi. Kidonda ya kijana huyu inapona vizuri. Lete vijiko saba na kisahani mbili. Hii chuma ya motokaa yangu. Choo inajaa ya kiroboto. Huyu mchawi, ona chura katika kifuko yake. Kichungo hii imeharibika, lazma kuchunga tena. Angalia kijana huyu, yeye bado kujua kaz, yake.

LOCATIVE CASE. P. 35.

Weka viatu yangu mlangoni. Bwana hapana kwake, amekwenda shambani. Twakwenda nyumbani kwetu, were kwenda kwako !

Labda nitajaribu kununua ndizi sokoni, kama siwezi kupata huko nitakwenda dukani. Alitoka mlimani, alipita mtoni, na kama nalimkutana alikimbia njiani. Tia kahawa mezani sebuleni. Alikuja kwangu na kipande yake mkononi. Naliona kifaru mbili uporini, nasikia kwamba umepiga kwa mkuke kifaru mingi musitoni mara nyingi. Mwambia mpishi kwamba nataka kuangalia jikoni. Anika nguo hii juani, lakini weka hii kivulini.

MA- CLASS NOUNS. P. 36 & 37.

Gari la moshi imekwisha fika. Sasa nitaandika mapatano yako. Miti ya malozi inazaa. Wapi majibu ya barua yangu ? Majivu nyeupe, lakini makaa nyeusi. Chukua shoka hii na toa maganda ya miti ile na tia katika pipa ile. Umesahau kuleta bakuli. Huyu mgonjwa ya tumbo (or tumboni). Tupa chupa. Waona gari ile na ngombe kumi na sita ? Lete makaa kuanza moto. Bwana twataka kujenga kanisa shambani. Umevunja mayai yote mara ingine, wapi masikio na macho yako ? Wacha maneno, makosa yako tu. Lokota maua na matunda yote na peleka kwangu. Jembe imeharibika. Jembe majani hii tu. Wewe, kwenda sokoni ya kununua maziwa na mafuta ya taa, 'sababu mimi nakwenda kwa makusanyiko ya wazungu. Nani wewe ? Mimi mutu tu ! Ndio lakini jina yako nani ? Wapi mikebe ya mafuta na sanduku ya sabuni ? Naona yote mbili mezani. Mimi mgonjwa shingoni. Natafuta mafuta ya jembe. Napenda machungwa sana, nipa chungwa moja, tena papayi na mananasi mbili. Jaza shimo yote shambani. Mtungi inajaa ya maji. Jua na nguvu sana, mawe moto kabisa. Bibi ya huyu analeta shauri bwana, shauri kidogo tu, hapana maneno mingi. Meno yake mzuri. Mlingote ya gari imevunjika. Fungua dirisha.

VERBS " TO BE " AND " TO HAVE." P. 38.

Iko ndizi shambani leo ? Ndio bwana iko, lakini mpishi amechukua yote ya kuiva na inabaki mbaya tu. Mbaya namna gani ? Ingine mbichi, ingine imekwisha oza, ile mzuri mpishi iko nayo nyumbani yake. Kwenda kwake na rudi naye, nataka maneno na mpishi, halafu labda nitakuwa na ndizi kwangu kesho. Ndizi matunda mzuri, mpishi ni mwivi. Juzi-juzi jembe ingine ilikosa, nitakuwa hapa kesho kutwa, lazma kuwa na chuma yote hapa, sababu nataka kuhesabu mara ingine, na mimi iko na shauri mingi kesho. Wewe iko na kisu, boy ? hapana bwana, wewe unayo. Hapana, sinayo.

ADVERBS AND PREPOSITIONS. P. 39.

Wajua kwamba jua ni juu yetu. Nitamwona baada ya chakula nyuma ya jikoni. Angalia mpishi, tangu nalikula mkate ile ulifanya, mimi mgonjwa sana, sababu wapika kibaya kabisa, tena wachelewa sikuzote, kama wafanya tena nitafukuza wewe kabisa. Waona nyumba ile huko chini kati-kati ya miti ? Nataka wewe kwenda huko sasa hivi, na upesi kabisa. Najua ni mbali, lakini zamani nalifika huko mara nyingi kwa saa moja. Nalikuwa mbeli, lakini ndugu yangu alikuwa nyuma. Mutu hapana kupata viatu bure kama ni viatu vizuri. Kazi yako bure tu. Bwana yako iko ndani ? Chupa ine ya maziwa hapana kutosha, kesho nitataka zaidi. Baba yako iko inje, karibu ya miti mkubwa, kwenda kuona, na halafu rudi ndani pamoja naye. Wasema kweli, iko nyumba kati-kati na miti kando-kando.

DERIVED ADJECTIVES. P. 40 & 41.

Nitakaa hapa peke yangu, lakini wewe mwenyewe, kama tayari, utakwenda, pamoja na mpishi, katika nyumba ya kizungu ile mlimani. Najua kweli kwamba ni ya zamani sana lakini ninyi mbili utasafisha na tengeneza sawa-sawa, sababu rafiki yangu atalala huko. Huyu mutu wa mali sana na apenda kila kitu safi na sawa-sawa, hapendi vitu ya kishenzi sawa-sawa masikini. Mupa maji ya moto tele na angalia wewe maridadi. Weka kitambaa ya dirisha rahisi ya amerikani na chukua nayo ile ya gali, tia ile ya rangi ya majani katika dirisha ya kushoto na ile ya buluu katika dirisha ya kulia, halafu kama yote tayari nipa habari, na nitakuja kuangalia. Mchungi ni baridi na ngombe yake ni maji-maji, lakini haithuru yeye kweli mutu na nguvu. Ngombe ya kwanza (or ya mosi) ni nyeusi, ile ya mwisho nyeupe, ile ya pili na ya sita nyekundu. Nilifanya mwezi wa jana.

TIME AND DAYS. P. 41 & 42.

Saa ngapi ? Saa tisa. Saa moja. Saa kumi na nusu. Saa moja na nusu usiku. Saa kumi na moja usiku. Saa sita usiku. Saa kumi na moja. Saa mbili. Saa tano. Saa ine ya nusu usiku. Saa kumi na mbili jioni. Saa kumi na mbili ya asubuhi.

Ninyi watoto mbili utachunga miti ya matunda mchana mzima, wewe utakuja asubuhi sana kama jua bado kuonekana, huyu atakuja saa sita mpaka usiku, wewe hapana kutoka mpaka huyu anafika. Kazi yako ya kufukuza ndege na kuangalia ndege hapana kula matunda. Ninyi mbili utafanya juma tatu, juma tano, jumaa, na juma pili ya wiki hii, na watoto ingine mbili watafanya juma ine, alhamisi, na juma mosi. Jana ilikuwa juma tatu, kesho kutwa itakuwa alhamisi. Mwaka huu (or hii) siku kuu itakuwa siku ya jumaa.

MONEY AND MEASURES. P. 44.

Nitatoa mshahara sasa, lakini ya kwanza nitawapa wanawake bakshishi yao ya debe ya kahawa wamevuna, senti kumi kila debe. Mwambia karani kuangalia kila debe ni ya kahawa ya kuiva tu. Kama mwana muke analeta debe na kahawa mbichi tele (or mingi) nitakataa bakshishi yake. Sasa wewe mzee, mshahara yako shilingi kumi, lakini umekwisha kukopa tatu, inabaki shilingi saba. Ngapi bwana ? Rupia tatu na nusu ! Mwambia neopara kutoa posho, bibi (or wana wake) ya debe tatu wapata kibaba mzima, lakini ile ya debe mbili wapata kibaba nusu, na ile ya debe moja tu hapana kupata. Ndito huyu ana debe mbili, senti ishirini, na bibi huyu, mama yake, iko na debe tatu, senti thelathini, nitawapa sumuni pamoja, sababu senti karibu kwisha. Shilingi sita na senti thelathini. Shilingi nane na senti ishirini. Shilingi ine na senti thelathini na tano. Shilingi kumi na moja na nusu (or sumuni). Shilingi tano na pesa nane. Shilingi kumi na tano na senti sabaini na tano. Senti sabaini na tano ni sumuni na pesa nane. Iko dudu tele hapa.

U- CLASS SUBSTANTIVES. P. 45.

Mzigo ya kwanza mzito, ile ya pili mzito sana, lakini ile ya tatu mzito kabisa. Wembe hii kali kuliko ile ; wasema nini ? nasema, wembe hii inashinda ile. Lete ufagio na fagia sebuleni, iko kuni chini. Hii kitambaa ya uso. Hii urongo yake tu bwana, aliiba unga kutengeneza uji au ugali yake. Nini ugonjwa yako ? (or Ugonjwa yako gani ?) Walala usiku ? Nionyesha ulimi yako. Sijui, wewe wathani nini ? Uchawi ? hapana, hii upuuzi tu. Piga randa mbau hii halafu kata kwa urefu hii, pima sawa-sawa ubau hii, kisha tumia kujenga ukuta huko. Wapi funguo ya sanduku hii ? Nataka kutafuta utambi. Kama watandika meza tia kisu upande ya kulia ya sahani, na uma upande ya kushoto. Wino imekauka. Upanga yako kali sawa-sawa wembe. Upepo imechukua uzi, lete ingine mrefu sana.

ENGLISH WORDS. P. 47.

Boy, tengeneza bafu yangu, na hapana kutia maji ya moto tele sawasawa (or kama) ulifanya jana, napenda moto, lakini hapana moto sana. Kufua nguo utataka sabuni, buluu, na sitachi, njoo kwa (or katika) sitoa na nitakupa, angalia kwamba shiti na blanketi yangu imekauka. Mwambia ndaraiva hapana kukaza feregi ya gari kabisa (or sana) nataka miguu kuweza kupindua. Wewe bado kumaliza futi yako nalipima, lazma kujembe laini ya binzi hii na saladi ile. Kabadi hii inanuka ya chizi, lete barasi na maji na sugua mbau yake. Nataka wewe kwenda kwa posta na barua hii, na kama wapita skulu njiani mupa mwalimu koti hii na soksi hii na fulana. Chukua barua hii kwa bwana nekitari kusema kwamba nataka kwinini ya watu kwa wiki ingine, labda utamwona katika jeli. Bwana mgeni ataka bisikoti na nimelete. Bwana nipa pini kutoa dudu ya mguu yangu. Lete kitabu yangu ya piksha na futi ile. Mwambia mpishi kuleta fraipani na tini-kata. Anapiga loboti kwamba peloti watapiga peksen ya nyumba yake.

FINAL EXERCISE. P. 50, 51 & 52.

Fundi ya matafali ametengeneza (or amefanya) tembo tele, anacheza karata na shemeji yake sermala. Mwambia neopara nataka kujenga nyumba (or kibanda) ya gari, wapi futi ? Lete kigingi ya kupimia (or kupima) mahali. Lete mitalimbo mbili ya kuchimba shimo ya miti. Hapana iko mitalimbo ? (or mitalimbo hapana iko ?) Haithuru (or basi) chonga miti minene mbili na tumia mahali ya mitalimbo. Peleka watu wawili musitoni kukata nguzo mrefu mbili na uma juu yake, na wawili wengine (or ingine) kukata fito, wawili kutafuta kamba, na wengine kukata majani, na wengine kukata miti. Halafu kesho toa debe mbili na jembe mbili na tia watu ine kukanyaga udongo, waweza kupata maji ya fereji ya maji. Nyani (or nyanya) wamekula binzi na maharagwe yote, lazma kuongeza boma ya shamba. Ndito ya karani ataka kununua ushanga, atauza kuku, iko arusi kesho kutwa. Wewe bado kulipa kodi yako, wewe kabila gani ? Nitatoa mshahara kesho jioni. Tembo wamekanyaga fereji na maji inatoroka. Bwana serikali alikwenda safari mwezi iliopita, na alipiga kiboko moja, kifaru mbili, kongoni tano, nkulu mbili, bongo saba, topi mbili, chui, impala, mbogo mbili na swara mingi ; aliona twiga na punda-milia mbili simba inaua, lakini ngozi yao iliharibika na fisi (or nyangau). Juma ine atakwenda kupiga mabata, kanga, na labda sangura. Wapagazi wake wamekula nyama mpaka wameshiba kabisa. Nasikia kwamba ngombe malaya amekufa, toa ngozi yake, nitakuja kuangalia moyo, figo, na ini. Mwambia fundi ya bau kuleta msumeno, patasi, sengenge, nyundo na misumari, na wewe mwenyewe kwenda kuleta sururu mbili. Gunia mbili hii ya posho inajaa ya dudu. Tia gunia ine hii ya mbego ya mahindi (or ya mahindi ya kupanda) katika kitanda na funika na chandarua. Mupa sais matandiko hii na mwambia kutandika frasi. Muhindi anaomba ruksa bwana. Panda miti ya ulaya hii karibu ya boma ya ngombe. Naona wajua kukama ngombe, wewe fundi sana. Bwana dakitari ya ngombe ataka kuchanja mtamba yote kesho. Tia maji ya ndimu na sukari kwa bilauri, koroga sana na mupa askari. Tengeneza kari jioni, unayo mchele, chumvi, pili-pili, na binzari ? Bwana, dobi analeta fitina kwangu, asema mimi naiba sharti, mshipi, suruali, na jozi mbili ya sokisi. Chukua pampa hii na ongeza pumuzi (or baridi, or hewa), kwa (or katika) mpira ya motokaa. Kama wataka kutahiri nitafuta kipande yako. Paka alikamata panya, lakini mbwa alimfukuza na panya aliteroka. Bwana, mimi mgonjwa ya homa, usiku nalitapika na nalitoa jasho tele, singizi hapana kamata mimi. Boy, wembe yangu imeharibika, hapana kukata hata kidogo, najua wewe umetumia ya kunyoa kichwa yako, na makasi yangu vile-vile, ni bado chafu na nywele nyeusi yako. Umejaza birika bure, imetoboka na chai imekwisha toroka yote. Panda miti hii kwa shimo hii, funika mizizi na mchanga na kanyaga, angalia ni imara halafu tia mavi (or cheroni) ya ngombe. Jogoo iko na dudu (or kiroboto) mingi, lete mafuta ya taa na maji ya kusafisha, basi, kidogo tu. Nyumbu ni mtoto ya frasi na punda. Miguu (or gurudumo) ya motokaa inapindua bure sababu iko matope mingi (or tele) tia nyororo. Kama nakupa wewe tumbako ya bakshishi lazma kusema asante. Nguruwe ya ulaya ameanguka shimoni (or kwa shimo), labda mbavu yake imevunjika. Fereji hii bei (or kiasi) gani ? Hii rahisi ? Hapana, imetoka ungereza, ni gali sana. Iko wazungu watatu inje, moja Kaburu na mbili Wangereza. Askari alikuja mapema na aliomba buni. Huyu pumbafu kabisa, hapana kujua kitu, afanya kila kitu goi-goi. Mtoto ya kukamata kamba ya kichwa ya ngombe aitwa mshika-kamba. Tia pumuzi ndani mpira hii. Njia karibu ya daraja mbaya sana, iko mchanga tele juu yake, toa mchanga na chimba fereji chini sana kando-kando yake. Bwana nataka kuhama, hapana bahati hapa, zamani bibi yangu alipata mimba lakini mara moja alipata mgonjwa sana, tumbo yake ilihara sana halafu mtoto alitoka, sasa hawezi mtoto, ni malaya tu, sasa nataka kwenda kwa shamba ya bwana mrefu, lakini shemeji yangu atakaa hapa ya kuchungia (or kuchunga) wimbi na mtama yangu. Hii nyumba ya kuku goi-goi, chui aweza kuvunja hii rahisi, kuku ya ungereza gali, nitajenga ingine ya mabati. Iko vumbi tele sana hapa, tupa maji juu yake, kama hapana mikebe ya maji, unayo kibuyu. Basi, nipa pesa nane, na nitakupa stampu, karatasi na bahasha.

Kesho asubuhi nitataka watu nane ya kazi ya rege-rege ya mahindi. Lazma kuweka visikoro huko, na nataka ndito mbili kuja kazi ya kutoa mahindi ya kubaki na mikono. Bwana, sheki-sheki ya rege-rege imeharibika, kichungo ya mabati imepotea. Basi, lazma kutuma watu wawili ingine kuchunga mahindi katika sheki-sheki ingine. Unayo petrol kutosha ya kupiga stat kwa tinka-tinka ya kusaga kahawa ? Hapana Bwana, fundi aliomba juzi-juzi ya piki-piki yake na nalimupa yote. Nkulu wamekula mahindi na nimepiga moja, ngozi itafaa ya kutengeneza sirupu mzuri na nitatengeneza misharidi ya ngozi ya shingo, iko mafuta ya uto ya kusugua katika kamba ? Tunayo kamba na terensi tele au lazma kusokota ngozi ingine ? Bau ya mtaragwa napasuka mepesi lakini hapana kupindua sana, lakini bau ya podo hapana kupasuka sana lakini inapindua sana. Iko hapa miti ya matamayo, chonga yoki sawa–sawa ile, nitarudi halafu ya kupima mahali ya kutoboa tundu ya kesikei na ya chuma ya yoki. Nitapanda makuyu ya kufunika miti ya kahawa kivulini yao.

MILITARY TERMS. P. 54.

Kesho utapeleka karutu katika shabaha. Watapiga katika hatua mia moja, angalia kwamba walinga sawasawa, na wakamua teriga taratibu. Wanayo risasi ngapi katika mabete yao? Kama adui watashambulia mji hii tutalinda handaki hii na bombom na bombu, tutatengeneza sengenge ya miba mbele, na tena mizinga itatupa baruti kwao. Burujee alichelewa ya kupiga mlio wa buruji. Askari yule amelewa, mfunga korokoroni na mlete maktab mabusu kesho. Anayo asanta, lakini sasa ametoka adabu anaharibu heshima ya Keyaa na athabu yake itakuwa mzito. Tia risasi kwa brich halafu shindilia na rama na tia maganda. Lea atalinga mzinga kwa darubini, na piga kwa stima. Simama sawasawa! Kaza mabega, tupa kifua, inua kidevu, nyosha magoti! Wewe namna gani? Ndio fanti, najaribu kufanya bidii lakini roho yangu imekufa. Shawesh moja na mbasha wawili na asikari kumi watakwenda manyata ile. Ya kwanza njia inakwenda kusini, inapita jangwa, na mikondo mbili, inapita mwamba mirefu na inapinduka mashariki, inaingia mbugani, halafu vishakani, halafu porini mpaka mtoni na ngambo yake iko mwitu. Iko kivuko ya kupita mto, na njia inapinduka kaskazini, inafuata bonde na katika mwisho yake iko mtaa ya mkikuyu. Wacha shamba yake katika upande ya kushoto yako na utafika katika kijiji, iko kisima huko. Mbele ya mji iko ziwa. Kama wasimama pwani na tezama baharini utaona maji tu mpaka upeo wa macho, lakini kama wakwenda mangaribi kwa meli kisiwa itaonekana karibu. Mtu wa raiya ameniambia kwamba ilikuwa mapigano jangwani jana. Ilikuwa silaha mingi chini, bunduki, singe, ala, mikoba, na aliokota dira na darubini. Risasi ni ya risasi na maganda ya shaba. Tegemea kisigino cha mkono katika goti yako. Katika laini iko watu wengi wanahara damu, wengine wana tego ao kisonono na kukojoa ni chungu. Ana jeraha katika kisigino cha mguu yake, tia katika machera. Hawezi kupiga ngumi ameuma konde yake. Watu wa tu tu kwa kulia, watu wa wan wan kwa kushoto. Peleka baruti hii katika kwota gaad. Baruti ilipasuka katika daraja kama watu wa msaada walidumu mji. Wewe hukufuata amri yangu, unayo makosa tano ya zamani, hukumu yangu kwamba utapoteza tepe yako. Utalinda baruti hii, sawasawa kanuni, mpaka tamaam. Mwambia kiongozi kukaza mshipi wa mabega yake. Wapagazi wamekula wali na tende yote, haithuru, tutapata mchele ingine kesho lakini labda itakuwa mpungu tu. Aliniamru kupiga tamaam. Alama yao ni nyota.

Zima taa ile! Sabmarini mbili ya adui ilizama kwa baruti ya manowari yetu, lakini ya kwanza walizamisha meli mbili yetu. Mwambia mlinzi (or sentri) ya mizinga hapana kuwacha mutu kukaribia (or kuja karibu) baruti na sigara, sababu hatari sana. Tuma N.C.O. na watu sita kupeleleza mpaka juu ya mlima ile. Nimeharifu kwamba iko ta mjini. Usisonga (or hapana kusonga) kama wapiga maktaim !